DEVELOPING SELF-ESTEEM

DEVELOPING SELF-ESTEEM

How to Overcome Fear and Anxiety
and Regain Confidence

Alexandra Strong

A PRACTICAL GUIDE TO
IMPROVING SELF-ESTEEM AND CONFIDENCE

DEVELOPING SELF-ESTEEM

How to Overcome Fear and Anxiety and Regain Confidence

COPYRIGHT

©2015 by Alexandra Strong

All rights reserved. No part of this publication may be reproduced in any form or by any means, including scanning, photocopying, or storing it in any medium by electronic means without prior written permission of the copyright holder.

ISBN-13: 978-1530060108

ISBN-10: 1530060109

DISCLAIMER

The publisher and the author make no representation or warranties with respect to the accuracy or completeness of the contents of this work and specifically disclaim all warranties, including without limitation warranties of fitness for a particular purpose. No warranty may be created or extended by sales or promotional materials. The advice and strategies contained herein may not be suitable for every situation. This work is solid with the understanding that neither the publisher nor the author is engaged in rendering legal, accounting, or other professional services. If professional assistance is required, the services of a competent professional person should be sought. Neither the publisher nor the author shall be liable for damages arising here from. The fact that an organization or website is referenced in this work as a citation and/or a potential source of further information does not mean that the author or the publisher endorses the information the organization or website may provide or recommendations it may make. Further, readers should be aware that internet websites listed in this work may have changed or disappeared between the date this work was written and when it is read.

TABLE OF CONTENTS

Copyright

Disclaimer

Table of Contents

Understanding Self-Esteem

    Inner Eye

    How the Inner Eye Becomes the Inner "I"

    Self-Esteem in Five Questions

Self-Esteem Theories

    Theories Concerning Self-Esteem

    Abraham Maslow's Theory of Human Motivation

    The Sociometer Theory of Self-Esteem

    The Terror Management Theory of Self-Esteem

    Types of Self-Esteem

    High vs Low Self-Esteem

    Secure vs. Defensive

    Explicit, Implicit, Narcissism, and Egotism

Characteristics of Low Self-Esteem

    How to Identify Low Self-Esteem

High Self-Esteem

    Outward Characteristics of High Self-Esteem

    Confidence

    Self-Direction

Non-blaming Behavior

An Awareness of Personal Strengths

An Ability to Make Mistakes and Learn From Them

An Ability to Accept Mistakes from Others

Optimism

An Ability to Solve Problems

An Independent and Cooperative Attitude

Feeling Comfortable With a Wide Range of Emotions

An Ability to Trust Others

A Good Sense of Personal Limitations

Good Self-care

The Ability to Say No

Low Self-Esteem

How Low Self-Esteem Affects Us All

Depression: A Dangerous State in Which To Be

Being easily hurt

Anger: Recognize It and Express It

Frustration: An Essential Part of Life

Anxiety: A Cornerstone of Esteem

Shame and Guilt: The Quintessential Emotions

How Low Self-Esteem Affects Us (Thoughts)

Negative Self-Critical Thoughts

Unhelpful Thinking habits

The Effect of Low Self-Esteem On General Welfare

Physical Effects of Low Self-Esteem

Way of Life to Improve Self-Esteem

How Do You Feel About You?

Rosenberg Self-Esteem Scale

State Self-Esteem Testing

Building Self-Esteem

Self-Esteem Development

The Real You vs The False You

Read/Watch Inspirational Stories

Control your emotion

Liberation from Guilt

Conquering Your Inner Critic

How to Leave Insecurity Behind

Pursuing Happiness and Finding Your Joy

Learning How to Love Yourself

Developing Your Character and Spirituality

The Power of Beliefs

Looking to the Future

You Can Change

Practice, Practice, Practice

Using Affirmations to Change Your Thinking

Strengths and Weaknesses: Figuring Them Out

Using Affirmations to Change Your Thinking

Removing Negative Thinking

How to Talk To Yourself for Positive Results

The lives of others: Stop comparing yourself

Land Of Hope and Glory:

Don't Beat Yourself Up

Take Responsibility

Hold Yourself to Account

Beware of Overstretching Yourself

Setting Limits as a Key to Developing Self-Esteem

Making Commitments and Following Through

Know Where to Direct Your Focus

Here's to Me!

Focusing on Self Discipline

Reducing Your Stress Level

Use Mindfulness Meditation

The Big Picture

Life Skills

Are You Smiling Yet?

Stop and Smell the Roses

What Goes Around

Have a Little Fun

Develop a Passion

Reward Your Achievements

Take Responsibility

Healthy Lifestyle

Introduction to the Secret of Self-Esteem

Exercise and Endorphins

Mirror on the Wall

Postures of the Higher Self

You Are What You Eat

Healthy Relationships

Building Healthy Relationships with Others

Helping Someone in Need

How Volunteering Boosts Self-Esteem Levels

The Unique You

Seeking Professional Help

Low Self-Esteem: When to Seek Professional Help

Emotional and Behavioral Disorders

How to Treat It Professionally

UNDERSTANDING
SELF-ESTEEM

Inner Eye

Self-esteem is one of the essential elements of humanity and its relative strength or weakness determines much of how each of us lives and moves around in the world. It is a common topic among the armchair quarterbacks of our lives as well as clinical and research psychologists. In fact it is such a common topic, that most people think they know all about it; many of those same people would be surprised by what they don't know if they delved very far into the real theory and practice of self-esteem.

It's worth a detailed look, in short. Every person could benefit from gaining greater knowledge of what self-esteem is and what it isn't. What are the components of self-esteem? What theories have psychologists developed to explain how it plays out in the world? What does low self-esteem look like and what are its main characteristics? What might be some tools or techniques to help a person develop stronger self-esteem?

These are the questions we will explore below. Reading onward will equip you to examine your own life, from the sources of your current state of self-esteem to tips you might be able to use yourself or with others. You may even identify some characteristics in yourself that change your opinion as to the strength of your own self-esteem. We will begin by identifying the major components of self-esteem and how they play out in people's lives.

How the Inner Eye Becomes the Inner "I"

Perception may not be reality in many important parts of life (tax forms, for instance), but reality is nothing but our own perception when it comes to a key component of our ability to understand the world around us, our capacity for affection, and our very happiness. Self-esteem is nothing but our perception of ourselves, and it is a very potent reality.

Consider the memorable personalities of your past: the guy in your junior year who was so smart, so funny, and so good looking, but no one could stand to be around him for long because he couldn't take a joke on himself to save his life, let alone take a bit of helpful advice.

There was the beautiful woman you met after college who might have been a model, or she might have been a famous actress, who always had guys ready to ask her out, but, when you tried to get her to think beyond being a hostess at a strip-mall restaurant, she just started crying and wouldn't stop.

There was the guy you knew who had always wanted to be an engineer, and who just fell apart when he got a B in physics, and has never gotten his act together since then. But when you got a B- in physics, it didn't scare you for life.

Then there's the woman who cleans the office: no one else is more fun or easier to talk to at the end of the day, and, when she's gone, you find yourself wishing you were half as easy in your skin as she is.

For good or for ill, self-esteem shapes who we are, how we interact with other people, and how we chart the course of our lives. If someone's self-esteem is too high, there's no way for that person to hear criticism productively. Their assessment of themselves is so far beyond reason that it has to be defended to an unreasonable extent.

If someone's self-esteem is too low, criticisms and insults, even baseless ones, are affirmations of their own skewed self-value, and, strangely, praise can be as distressing and bitter as criticism can be to someone with a swollen head.

Self-worth is usually focused on certain aspects of one's self. We watch certain parts of our lives as benchmark indicators of our overall value. A lawyer who gets crushed in court will still keep his chin up if he can see clearly that he was fighting a weak case. Besides, he's only an attorney to cover the expenses of being an excellent skier.

Self-esteem that is just right may very well be the best path to a happy life that there is. Arthur Miller said that the best basis for a tragedy was when a man's estimation of himself was radically higher or lower than the estimation of the world around him. Self-esteem that finds the middle ground would seem to enable one to be about as happy living in a mansion with a private beach as in a duplex with cockroaches.

Self-Esteem in Five Questions

- Who am I?
- Who loves me?
- What am I able to do well?
- What do I want to accomplish?
- Who will be with me if I fail?

What worries me, and how much?

To get a quick and easy overview of what's involved in self-esteem, consider these questions. Answered thoughtfully, seriously, and candidly, each one gives a key insight into each of the five elements of self-esteem.

Selfhood is the sense of being one's own person, and having a sense of one's own characteristics. Robust self-esteem is grounded in the accuracy of one's self-awareness. It does far more harm than good for someone to believe that he is a great opera singer when he is, in fact, mediocre at best when judged by the usual standards. On the other hand, someone might have sturdy self-esteem and a firm sense that they are a fine singer—in the way they want to be, and it is a great pity that more people don't appreciate their style of singing. Responsibility, or ownership of one's own actions, is a key part of this.

Affiliation is that sense that one has a secure and valued place in a community, be it a family, a workplace, a school, or a club. Every branch of anthropology, however at variance otherwise, has confirmed the vital role of social interaction and affirmation for humans in every stage of development. To borrow from an old sitcom's introduction, we all need to know that there's a place where everybody knows our name, and they're always glad we came.

Competence is the sense that one has skills and abilities that are valuable. "What am I good for?" is another way of asking the question for which this element of self-esteem provides the answer. Like all of the other ingredients, this one is linked to the others; people must not only be aware of their abilities, but also know that these abilities are valued by those around them. You don't necessarily need Rachel Ray to say so in order to believe that you can cook pretty well. But you do need to hear it from the people who provide your affiliation, if cooking is going to become a competence that grounds your self-esteem.

Mission, closely related to competence, is the sense that, not only is there something that we can do, there is something that we need to do. Everyone has seen what this can do to someone's self-esteem. Think of how someone who has failed again and again can have faith in themselves enough to try again because they have something they're determined to do—and when they don't—the person who has so little opinion of themselves, however great their accomplishments, will still have no idea what they want to do. They will say, "I will try again," which is so critical to a sense of what one can do because it can only proceed from a desire to accomplish something.

Finally, there is security, or the sense that the safety net which affiliation provides is a durable one. Few can believe in their own abilities or set out to accomplish what their heart desires when they are worried that those they love will abandon them if they fail. But how often have we seen—and been elated to see—what a person can do who knows that she has a friend who will be cheering her on, whether she is the first across the line or the last.

Who Am I? Internal Control, Intrinsic Motivation, and Selfhood in Self-esteem

The first major component of self-esteem that we will examine in detail can be variously called "selfhood" or the possession of internal self-control. A healthy sense of self-esteem requires a firm knowledge of one's self – not just the basic details, but the ability to thoroughly answer the question, "Who am I?" and to do so accurately. Self-control and an inclination toward personal responsibility are essential elements of the sort of full selfhood that is involved in robust self-esteem.

It is easy to have part of this sense of self and to appear to have an elevated self-esteem when, in fact, the walls are crumbling to dust all around you. Consider the case of a young man who has, from childhood, identified himself as a scientist. He was fascinated from the age of four by topics such as volcanoes, biochemistry, applied medicine and astrophysics. A precocious reader and student, everything in his educational context plus parental encouragement helped him to develop this vision of himself. He pushed himself to master the mathematics required to pursue his scientific interests and accelerated through and beyond the standard school curriculum.

He felt good about himself and his accomplishments. He seemed to be comfortable in the community of self-proclaimed science and math geeks that he had become part of. His self-esteem appeared to be strong. It was more surprising when toward the end of his high school career and the beginning of college, his internal vision began a dramatic shift and he lost his self-confidence and pride in himself. Several factors contributed to the change. He realized that he was merely going through the motions of interest in topics that had formerly intrigued him. While he was still quite competent, he'd lost the zeal that had previously characterized his work.

Once that was gone, he suddenly doubted everything about himself. He realized that he had allowed his parents and teachers to shape his interests and to take responsibility for large sections of his life that he was too busy and academically oriented to pay any heed to. He began to see that his sense of control over his life had been artificial because it was externally applied and didn't proceed naturally from his own internal vision of himself. Now he was left in the ruins of what he had imagined were his own goals, and he didn't even have the skills he thought he'd need to develop a new self. Is it any wonder that his self-esteem melted away? It had been grounded in quicksand, not in the firm ground of internal motivation and personal responsibility.

A rough year or two intervened, but eventually he emerged a stronger, more balanced person with a firmer sense of self-esteem than ever before. He stopped making excuses for himself, learned some essential life skills with the help of his friends, and turned his focus from doing what the outside world expected of him into doing what his own true self demanded. Now he is interning with an architecture firm and writing poetry on the side – catching up in many areas and rueful about what he considers lost opportunities, but taking responsibility for his own future in an unprecedented way and happier than he's been since he was constructing model volcanoes on his parents' kitchen floor. His self-esteem is growing, and this time it is at a more appropriate level and much more likely to stick around because it is founded on a firm sense of self and his place in the world.

No Man (or Woman) is an Island: Affiliation and Self-Acceptance

"Were you raised by wolves?"

This classic rebuke provides an unintended insight into how deeply important other people's feedback is for us. Assigning the source for outlandishly uncouth behavior to a lack of social feedback in childhood seems symmetrically and humorously outlandish, but the joke needs no explaining.

We know intuitively that most of our norms for behavior come from our observations of others' actions and reactions. From birth, we need and desire positive reactions to our own behavior from those around us. We are forming affiliations before we know how to speak or walk, finding our people and drawing comfort and support from feeling wanted and appreciated. When we are surrounded by people who themselves have healthy self-esteem, this leads to a virtuous cycle of acting in ways that promote one's own self-esteem and getting reinforcement that reinforces and further encourages this behavior.

When children find themselves in families and among friends who honestly encourage each other and respect each other's' differences, they feel more secure in taking risks without fear of rebuke or disapproval if they fail and are more ready to nurture their own individual qualities and strengths than those who, by observing how their families and friends treat each other, have learned to dread rebukes and ridicule.

Like warmth from a stove, high self-esteem tends to engender high self-esteem by proximity in early childhood, and life-long tendencies take root. Genuinely encouraging environments to provide children with the security to try new activities, make new friends, and to try zigging when everyone else is zagging. We need a sense of affiliation to promote our self-esteem, but we also need to love ourselves as individuals and accept who we are.

The last element is a most intriguing paradox in self-esteem:

Confident individualism seems to stem, at least at first, from the assurance that one will still be accepted by those around you if you do things differently from them. Many of the crises of adolescence are due to viewing affiliation and self-acceptance as separate things, and attaching self-esteem solely to one or the other. As we grow to adulthood, if we are fortunate, we learn that they must be blended as part of true self-esteem.

If you've found the correct affiliation, it's based in things you love and are passionate about. If then, you're engaged in what you love to do, feel, or think about, you'll find that you're suddenly happier about yourself. The source of self-acceptance is in allowing the self to find its best expression in what it loves to do. In this way, all the components of self-esteem come together – selfhood and personal responsibility lead to comfort in the best group affiliations and to acceptance of yourself as you are, all of which leads you toward self-efficacy and competence in your chosen tasks. If we can bring ourselves this far, we have an excellent opportunity to develop lasting self-esteem and, consequently, effectiveness in doing well, and in doing good, in the world.

Yes, I Can! Competence as a Component of Self-esteem

As we've seen, an accurate self-awareness and self-control as well as a true sense of belonging and self-appreciation are essential elements of healthy self-esteem. But as much as it's nice to think that those elements are enough, there's another factor that plays a major role in self-esteem. That is competence or self-efficacy – how good you think you are at the things you do, and how accurate that self-assessment is.

The young man who got himself all wrong and left science behind for architecture is a cautionary tale when it comes to competence – it's not sufficient in and of itself. He was very good at the math and science he abandoned, but his developing internal control and sense of self demanded that he make his way into fields that better suited his true self. Yet as he was coming to this conclusion, his self-efficacy slipped several notches. He started missing details in his work because he wasn't that interested in it, so he came to incorrect conclusions. Doubt fed on doubt until he had convinced himself that he wasn't very good as a scientist and then, of course, he really wasn't!

Similarly, neither following in the path laid out by one's selfhood nor loving oneself and feeling a true sense of community in one's chosen activities is enough without competence. A young woman who has worked all her life to become a published writer might serve as an example of this fact. She has pursued writing out of a true sense of herself, and in pursuing this dream she has developed a strong sense of personal responsibility in working toward her goals. She has taken appropriate coursework and has practiced her craft daily. She's also good at meeting a self-imposed minimum number of pages to write daily, and she loves the work.

Furthermore, she loves the community of writers and fits in well with that group. Professors, fellow writers at retreats and conferences, and everyone who is interested enough to read her work at her day job, they all think she has some real talent and is a congenial person to have in the business. And she drinks in not only their approval, but the joy of being in their company. She is happy with herself, proud of her skills and creativity, and perfectly willing to accept that she'll never be a mathematician or statistician as long as she can keep writing fiction.

Yet, talented writer as she knows herself to be, her goal of becoming a published writer is elusive. There is an entire set of competencies requisite to achieving her goal that she has never been interested in or very good at. So, although she thinks she's an excellent writer and just the sort of person who ought to have a book contract and be entertaining proposals about the movie rights to her third novel, she can't get published in anything bigger than a minor literary journal. She has never been a salesperson or been much good at self-promotion, which are essential qualities in the publishing world. So her self-esteem takes a hit, not because she's wrong in her vision of herself or because she's excluded from a community, but simply because she didn't have a full picture of the competence she needed. Fully developed and strong self-esteem requires all of these components working in tandem. Sometimes all it takes is belief in oneself – after all, one can develop new competencies through repetition and practice.

SELF-ESTEEM THEORIES

Theories Concerning Self-Esteem:
Their Origin and Development

In the modern study of social psychology, much is made of self-esteem. Many researchers in the field have run controlled experiments and written many journal articles and books espousing their varying theories concerning self-esteem and its importance in human life and behavior. But, it was not always this way. How and why did self-esteem become such an important component of the field of psychology? To answer this question and begin to consider some of the main theories surrounding self-esteem, we must look back to the end of the nineteenth century and the dawn of the twentieth century.

Sigmund Freud and those he influenced, such as Carl Jung, had founded psychoanalysis and analytical psychology around the general concept that human behavior is influenced by factors within the human mind – Freud's unconscious mind and emphasis on changing behavior through talking about internal conflicts and difficulties, Jung's collective unconscious and integration of parts of the self in order to achieve wisdom and wholeness.

Partially in reaction to these thinkers, B.F. Skinner developed his theory of radical behaviorism, which was based upon the idea that none of Freud's or Jung's ideas about the effects of the unconscious mind on behavior could be proven. He attempted to develop a science of human behavior, positing that human behaviors and human actions were never dependent upon internal factors but were entirely based on the consequences that would come from those actions. One associates with him the Skinner box and, perhaps, parenting techniques that involved leaving babies to cry in their cribs. In terms of his influence on psychology and later development of self-esteem theories, it is most important to remember that Skinner's work denied the existence of human freewill and advocated a system of positive reinforcement to condition people to exhibit desired behaviors. Their internal processes, emotions and feelings, played no role in Skinner's work.

At around the same time, other psychologists and scientific thinkers were pioneering a path that would lead to the dominance of self-esteem theories toward the end of the twentieth century. While Skinner's theories led to some potential improvements in areas such as education, encouraging rewards for active participation in learning instead of rote instruction and coercive punishments, there were some major drawbacks as well. Skinner's work, of course, denied that anything outside of consequences for behavior could shape behavior. Following it literally could lead to a classroom in which marbles moved from the happy reward jar to the sad-faced, no reward jar based on student behavior, but in which there was no consideration of the needs or feelings of any of the students in the classroom.

So these other thinkers began to lead the study of human behavior back to a focus on the internal workings of the mind as a source or outcome of human behavior. When Abraham Maslow developed his hierarchy of needs as a theory of human motivation in the 1940s and beyond, physiological needs such as air, water and security were lower on his list than internal needs such as love, belonging, self-esteem and self-respect. As psychology has developed since the days of Maslow, many theories have focused on self-esteem and its relationship to human motivation and behavior. We will examine in more detail Maslow's work and two of the more important recent theories concerning self-esteem;

Mark Leary's Sociometer Theory and Sheldon Solomon's intriguingly named terror management theory.

Abraham Maslow's Theory of Human Motivation

Hierarchy of Human Needs

In 1943, Abraham Maslow first published a theory of human motivation that introduced his hierarchy of needs. In essence, he theorized that humans are motivated by various needs, both external and internal, and must address these needs in order to move to higher levels of personal development. While this hierarchy is generally represented in a pyramidal form that appears to separate the forms of human need absolutely and imply that the satisfaction of one need must precede attention to another, Maslow was clear from the beginning that the levels of need were somewhat fluid and could coexist in a person.

The most basic needs that Maslow saw as motivating human behavior were physiological (air, water, food, sleep, excretion) followed by safety needs (for security of person, property, family, health and the like). And there is certainly something to be said for these needs taking precedence over any others. It is difficult to be motivated by a desire to overcome prejudice or to develop respect for others when you don't have enough food to eat or a source of clean water. And yet the human spirit does exert itself in odd ways – refusing help in the way of food or money out of a sense that accepting it would diminish one's self-respect or the respect of others, or because it comes at the price of abandoning one's family.

The higher order needs in Maslow's hierarchy of needs are these:

Needs for love and belonging, including friends and family as well as intimate relationships; and esteem needs. The esteem needs include not only self-esteem and confidence, but actual accomplishments. Maslow recognized that baseless self-esteem could not lead to higher levels of personal development. In Maslow's theory, it was only after a person had addressed all of these needs that he or she could hope to achieve self-actualization.

Self-Actualization

Abraham Maslow defined self-actualization as the human desire to achieve full potential, to develop the self and the world into something better than they had been previously. This is clearly in opposition to the behaviorism of Skinner and others in which all human responses are conditioned by stimuli and operate without freewill, and it can also be set in contrast to the work of Freud and others in which their study and psychotherapy were based on the correction of psychological problems. Maslow sought to emphasize the positive and people's potential for greatness. He studied healthy people who seemed to have achieved a large measure of self-actualization, and found that they exhibited a number of similar qualities.

Self-actualization seemed to Maslow to involve interests in truth, goodness, beauty, justice, wholeness and perfection. Those who had achieved it also possessed, however, qualities such as uniqueness, spontaneity, and playfulness as they appeared to make their work simple and effortless. According to Maslow's theory, they were motivated to develop these qualities because they had largely disposed of their other needs.

In focusing on humans' potential for goodness, Maslow's work opened itself up to a few major criticisms. First, it was largely subjective in that he decided which people (Albert Einstein and others) embodied self-actualization. Second, Maslow himself was forced to admit that even when people's needs were met, they did not always proceed to pursue self-actualization. Yet Maslow's work was foundational in humanistic psychology and helped lead to a greater emphasis on self-esteem in the development of healthy, whole individuals who might be seeking to change the world.

The Sociometer Theory of Self-Esteem

In the late 1990s, psychologist Mark Leary published his sociometer theory to explain the functions of self-esteem. According to this theory, self-esteem developed through an evolutionary process as a gauge of how desirable one is to others. The sociometer is, as its name implies, a measure we take automatically of our social acceptance. Positive social feedback – the friend who includes you, even the waiter who smiles back and engages in small talk – produces a range of positive emotions that can be described as heightened self-esteem. In contrast, signs or even fears of social non-acceptance – an averted look or roll of the eyes from one friend to another when you're nearby – produce lowered self-esteem.

According to sociometer theory, low self-esteem is nature's way of provoking a change in your behavior in order to gain more social acceptance. High self-esteem and its positive emotional framework encourage you in the behavior that brought you social acceptance. The evolutionary model behind this theory holds that social acceptance is a key to survival for humans because a group provides protection for its members and because social acceptance, at least by one other person, is important for reproduction.

The sociometer theory can provide a glimpse into how positive and negative feedback on social acceptance can dramatically skew the self-esteem of a young person. A growing child is, in large part, attempting to learn how to behave; testing boundaries, seeing what the best behaviors are in order to fit into the group – which, in the case of a young child, is essentially defined as immediate family or household. If such a child continually receives negative social feedback for practically any behavior, he or she will emerge from childhood with no idea of how certain behaviors might help in pursuing social acceptance in a broadening group. Therefore, they will have no mechanism to raise their self-esteem when it has hit rock bottom.

Alternatively, a child may receive positive feedback for practically any form of behavior, golden or rotten. A parent who claims to be raising a child's self-esteem by finding any way to praise him, even when he knocks another child down on the playground or screams at Aunt Edith is, indeed, raising his self-esteem. His parents are his social group, and the positive feedback is measured by inflated self-esteem. The snag comes when this child grows out of the tight family group into a larger social context. Suddenly unacceptable behaviors are met with negative reactions. Suddenly his self-esteem is tumbling, and he has no context for how to use that drop on the sociometer gauge to adjust his behavior and bring it back into an acceptable range for social acceptance.

Criticisms of the sociometer theory are often related to this last point – the theory would suggest that lowering self-esteem through negative social feedback should spark behavioral changes to facilitate repaired relationships and improved self-esteem. Instead, people with low self-esteem often remain chronically low in self-esteem or, worse, become aggressive or self-destructive. Leary and his colleagues point out in response that many of these behaviors are an attempt to gain acceptance gone wrong – substance abuse as an attempt to avoid rejection or find a new social group, for example – and that other theories have similar difficulty in fully explaining all aspects of self-esteem.

The Terror Management Theory of Self-Esteem

Sheldon Solomon and his co-authors introduced the terror management theory of self-esteem in 1991, a few years before the sociometer theory was published. In 1997, Solomon and others criticized the sociometer theory, saying that it did not match up to a growing body of evidence in favor of their own favored terror management theory. Then, what is this terror management theory? Is it as, well, terrifying as its name implies?

The idea behind terror management theory is that humans experience a psychological conflict between the desire to live and the knowledge that death will come. This conflict produces terror or anxiety that can be managed if a person attaches himself to a set of cultural values that give meaning to life. Self-esteem, according to this theory, is a personal metric of how well you are measuring up to your cultural values, and so it acts as a damper for death-linked anxiety by connecting you to things that give your life meaning.

Imagine Sharon, a woman in her mid-fifties. She is healthy and reasonably fit and has no particular reason to dwell on her own mortality. Most of the time, she doesn't. But if the theory holds, then Sharon will react in some fairly predictable ways when the thought of death does come up. As it happens, Sharon runs into her friend Frank at the grocery store. In the course of their conversation, he tells her that his friend and neighbor Tracey has just been diagnosed with an aggressive cancer and isn't expected to live more than six months. Sharon commiserates with Frank, but is soon lost in her own contemplations more than she is in his real sorrow for his friend. You see, Sharon knows Tracey, and knows that she's a few years younger than herself. Sharon can't stop turning it all over in her mind.

In the next few days, Sharon finds herself drawn to some activities that aren't in her usual repertoire. She goes to church on the weekend, something she hasn't much done in five years. She finds herself singing as she washes the dishes, only half-aware of what she's doing until she realizes she's singing songs that her mother taught her as a child. And she takes in a stray cat, though she doesn't really know why she has done it – she finds that she enjoys having something that she can call her own and put out when she doesn't want to deal with it.

Most interestingly, Sharon finds herself feeling better – more in touch with the world of her childhood and early adulthood, and somehow more in control of her own circumstances. She has put aside her anxieties by retreating into culturally familiar territory and by exerting her human power in relation to a small animal. More than that, she feels better about herself, like a person who is worth a great deal to the world at large. A reminder of her own mortality has spawned some changes in Sharon's behavior, and her self-esteem has risen. She has used these new positive feelings to put all those death-related thoughts far from her mind. This is all in accordance with the precepts of the terror management theory, which is, perhaps, not as alarming a theory as its name suggests.

Types of Self-Esteem

When we talk about self-esteem, we usually have in mind some complex attitude or a set of these, which every person possesses, and which defines this person's behavior, relationships, and social standing. Confidence, attitude towards personal strengths and mistakes, ability to make conscious decisions and much more are both components of self-esteem and results of a particular type of self-esteem. Below are some of the most popular classifications.

High and Low Self-Esteem

A lot has been said and written about these two dimensions. Although they often seem to be abstract concepts, there are trusted questionnaires which measure the level of self-esteem in people. These two types are often correlated with success and failure, correspondently, and require a separate article to be explained.

Adaptive and Maladaptive Self-Esteem

Adaptive self-esteem is associated with a person's using of inner resources, such as motivation, ability to work hard, reasoning, and many more, which facilitate self-development. Sense of authenticity derives from here too. Such people adapt to the new circumstances while always remaining themselves. Maladaptive self-esteem is positively correlated with others and the way in which others perceive an individual. Sense of superiority (usually together with extreme feeling of insecurity) evolves together with the development of maladaptive, externally looking self-esteem.

Worthiness-Based and Competence-Based Self-Esteem

These types might resemble the previous two. Let us look at the first one of them. Here are all the people whose self-esteem stems from their preoccupation with their worth in society or community. They can either be arrogant and authoritative, or they can be extremely hard-working or, for example, unable to say "no" to others. Competence-based self-esteem in individuals is associated with their life experience and is usually measured by individual achievements. While in the first case evaluation comes mostly from outside, in the second one it is carried out by the person him- or herself based on personal characteristics and work input/output.

Secure and Defensive Self-Esteem

These two types are also not this far from the previous two pairs (adaptive & maladaptive and worthiness-based & competence-based). The similarity lies within the fact that all these types represent people who are either subject to external opinions or who base their self-perception on internal factors. What concerns secure self-esteem; it is attributed to those who believe in themselves and their abilities, who are confident in their judgment and beliefs. Such people are indeed 'secure' on their own. On the opposite side, there are vulnerable individuals who are always looking for approval from others. It might even seem that they are searching for a way to defend their right to exist, while either being ready to fight for their beliefs (instead of having confidence in them) in front of others, or willing to subside rather than confront others.

Self-esteem is simply people's way of seeing themselves. Self-perception is in the core of self-esteem. After looking at the popular typologies of self-esteem, we may draw conclusions that it is related to a person's autonomy and their ability to evaluate, and also value, him- or herself without much concern for what others would think of them.

High vs Low Self-Esteem

When we are dealing with the concept of self-esteem, we are, in fact, talking about the measurements of one's perception of oneself, which determines a person's correlation of success and failure. Everything is simple; people with higher self-esteem are more likely to succeed, whereas those with low self-esteem undergo failures more often. The difference between those two types is great, but the line defining the 'height' of one's self-esteem is rather thin. However, there are personal attributes which, if true, define men and women with that necessary component of success, high self-esteem.

Self-confidence is an attribute of those who have values and beliefs of their own. People with low self-esteem will often subside or, on the contrary, defend their values and beliefs with extreme passion. At the same time, individuals with high self-esteem will use reasoning to defend their beliefs, but are always ready to adjust them to the more reasonable views of others.

People with high self-esteem will accept their strengths and weaknesses, as well as any limitation of their abilities. Low self-esteem would be a case of either those who are blind to their weaknesses or those who fail to see their strengths. High self-esteem means that people are able to make their own choices based on their judgment and experience. They are usually autonomous in making decisions and taking actions. On the other hand, it is only those with low self-esteem who are afraid to ask for help.

The higher the self-esteem, the more likely individuals are able to accept a range of feelings and emotions as part of their personalities. They keep those private when needed or they share them with others when it is appropriate. This is where their empathy towards others comes from and their conscious choice to live in harmony within society and follow its basic rules. High self-esteem is also associated with one's belief in equality of all people, in terms of rights and attitude. Such people neither look down upon others, nor do they consider others superior. At the same time, they accept the individual differences between everybody.

Belief in their own value to others is also an important trait of those with high self-esteem. They do not allow the dependency on others, but rather they engage in cooperation with others. They never let others manipulate them.

People with high self-esteem are interesting to communicate with, as they tend to have a range of interests and are able to enjoy multiple activities, often at the same time. They are smart enough to put just about the right amount of psychological resources into their attitude towards the past and the future. Individuals with low self-esteem often wallow in the past regretting about certain things; worrying about the days to come also applies to them. Those with high self-esteem live in the present; they learn from the past and plan for the future.

The difference between two people with high and low self-esteem is always visible in their posture and the manner of speech, as well as in their openness to others and open-mindedness to new ideas and thoughts. Fortunately, it is never too late to start learning from the former to become more confident, successful and looked up to.

Secure vs. Defensive

The expression "defensive self-esteem" is described as those times when, in an effort to feel better about ourselves, we shore ourselves up against any negative influences.

In simple terms this could be where someone chooses not to buy sweets in an effort to stay thin because it helps enhance that person's positive image of themselves.

Another example may be someone choosing not to associate themselves with any of their mischievous peers so they feel more worthy - even though these naughty ones may in fact be the ones that excel in class.

There is a growing body of research that those people with defensive self-esteem are more "fragile" than those with secure self-esteem.

This is significant because for many years it was thought that just having any self-esteem meant good self-esteem.

It is now recognized that some people with defensive self-esteem can display aggression and others can become unpleasant when their egos are perceived to be threatened.

Self-esteem is still regarded in the mainstream as a valuable component that is part of leading a productive and happy life, but more research is beginning to recognize that self-esteem can turn from being good to being bad.

One way self-esteem turns bad is when verbal defenses accompany it - when, for example, a person lashes out at those that threaten his or her beliefs, opinions, values, or statements.

One piece of research, that used 100 undergraduate students, split the study into three segments. In the first, the undergrads filled in a questionnaire and took part in other methods of evaluating their self-esteem. In the second, the students were assessed for their self-esteem's stability. The third involved an interview with each of the students to measure how much they verbalized their defensiveness.

The findings concluded that those people with low self-esteem tended to be more defensive verbally than those with high self-esteem.

Those people whose self-esteem was high are comfortable in their own bodies, happy with themselves - including any of their perceived faults. As these people feel threatened less, they tend not to resort to defensive language and don't blame others or make excuses about any transgressions or experiences that have ever threatened them.

One reason this research is considered important is because it emphasizes that increased vocalized defensiveness appears to relate to lesser psychological wellbeing and consequently has a detrimental effect on getting satisfaction from life.

The findings demonstrate that defensiveness is a reflection of fragility, insecurity, and suboptimal functioning rather than a psychological stance that is healthy.

This is not to suggest that there's anything wrong with those people who feel good about themselves. What it is suggesting is that those people that make it a prime directive to feel good about themselves are likely to subsequently reveal behaviors that are defensive and self-promoting. This has very limited benefit psychologically.

Explicit, Implicit, Narcissism, and Egotism That Feels Threatened

The expression "implicit self-esteem" is a reference to how we choose to evaluate ourselves in a positive or negative way. We do this in ways that are automatic, spontaneous, or even unconscious. The contrast with the expression "explicit self-esteem" is that this latter requires a more reflective and conscious evaluation of ourselves. However, both of these form our overall self-esteem as a whole.

Narcissism, on the other hand, describes how we may display a love for ourselves that is excessive. This is often demonstrated by an overinflated view of our self-worth. There is a correlation between self-esteem and narcissism but it is only moderate. It is possible for one of us to have both high self-esteem and low narcissism, and vice versa. Narcissists can display threatened egotism when they respond to any criticism that threatens their ego. This reaction can often and all-too-easily manifest itself in an aggressive or hostile way.

Implicit self-esteem suggests that our self-evaluation leaks into the objects we choose to have around us. This can be both unconscious and automatic. Several pieces of research have indicated that the level of implicit self-esteem can be adjusted by evaluation and associated conditioning.

Also making social comparisons, or measuring ourselves against others in our circles, may have a big effect on our implicit self-esteem. Our levels of implicit self-esteem affect us in a variety of circumstances - socially, emotionally, and in regards to our cognitive wellbeing. In a few cases, differences between our explicit and implicit self-esteem affects our wellbeing and can be associated with symptoms of a clinical nature. Our implicit self-esteem helps to determine how we approach conflicts in our relationships and in other social circumstances.

The discrepancies between explicit and implicit self-esteem have been variously described as self-esteem that is damaged if the explicit self-esteem is lower, and defensive self-esteem if the explicit self-esteem is higher. Indeed, it has been discovered in research tests that individuals trust their intuition when they lean more towards having a higher communication between their implicit and explicit self-esteem.

Differences in gender have been shown to play a pivotal role in how implicit self-esteem is influenced by how other partners perform. Women are also more likely to demonstrate a trust for their intuition and feelings, when compared to men. The relationship between implicit and explicit self-esteem is much less for men than it is for women.

While implicit self-esteem is seen to contain empirical and instinctive elements, those of us who are said to be in touch with our feelings are able to record higher explicit self-esteem. Studies have supported this assertion.

CHARACTERISTICS OF LOW SELF-ESTEEM

How to Identify Low Self-Esteem When You See It

So much discussion of self-esteem centers on high self-esteem or how to develop higher self-esteem; we all have some idea of what good self-esteem looks like or feels like when observed in another or oneself. In consequence, though, we may have lost track a bit of what low self-esteem is or what it looks like to the observer. Let us review some of the most important characteristics of low self-esteem, as knowing what they are will make it easier for us to approach a discussion of how to increase our self-esteem.

Negative view of life

You have probably known this character. He's always sighing when others are laughing, he has nothing positive to say, and he seems to think that the world is against him. Of course, on some occasions, it may be. There's usually some basis in personal history for a negative outlook on life. Perhaps his weight, or his accent, or his disability turned his community somewhat against him as a child. He didn't fit in, and so he retreated deep within himself to avoid the pain of rejection.

As he matured, he began to emerge, but only to snap at the world in general. Government is bad, foreign nations are no better, imported diseases are going to kill us all, it's never going to rain again unless a tornado comes – this is the stuff of his conversation, such as it is. It is important to remember that his self-esteem is low because of his past difficulties, and he has not grasped the tools he needs to raise it. A negative outlook on life is one of several factors that often points out a person with low self-esteem to an observer.

Perfectionist attitude

This characteristic of low self-esteem is a bit less obvious. What's wrong with doing good work consistently? Why would that mean that someone has low self-esteem? In fact, taking pride in the quality of one's work might be considered a mark of high self-esteem. It is important to look beyond the apparent pride in personal work in order to consider the sources of the perfectionist attitude as well as its expression.

There are certainly people who take great and appropriate care about their work and yet feel good about themselves and their place in the world, showing signs of high self-esteem. But the truly perfectionist impulse usually springs from a lack, rather than an abundance, of confidence. The perfectionist may have been chastised earlier in life for a lack of planning or slipshod results. Or, perhaps the work was always good, and the perfectionism springs from fears about others' appreciating its author and concerns that allowing any flaw will lead to a complete unraveling of the status the perfectionist has won through hard work.

Think about how perfectionism is typically expressed. Is the perfectionist truly proud of her work? Or does she, instead, present each golden, glowing product half-heartedly, as if waiting for someone to criticize it? Does she downplay her excellence? Does she never stop working long enough to take any credit, but always move right on to the next thing? If this is her pattern, then her perfectionism is likely to be a shield. It may be protecting her from social interactions that make her uncertain and uncomfortable, or it may mask a real lack of confidence in her abilities. In either case, low self-esteem is often at the heart of perfectionist tendencies.

Mistrust of others

We all have our moments of not trusting other people. If we're intuitive people, then we're likely to be right most of the time – we might spot a real villain lurking in sheep's clothing. But have you ever known a person who always seems to lack trust in other people, even those who are honestly trying to express real affection? This is a fairly certain indicator of a person with low self-esteem.

Jim is one of these people. He never quite believes what anyone tells him, especially if it has to do with him, and especially if it's favorable. Oddly, it's the people reaching out to him in friendship who get the least trust in response. Jim is gay, and when he was in high school he wasn't out publicly, but he was continually harassed because his fellow students presumed that he was gay. Jim's worst memories of high school involve boys who acted interested in him only to quickly turn against him and ridicule him publicly. It's fairly clear why Jim stopped putting trust in his fellow man!

Thirty years have passed, and Jim is in a committed relationship now, but getting there was a struggle. He had come to the conclusion that the end of humankind is self-interest, and that those who showed interest in him were actually out for something for themselves. Whether it was sex, money, employment, or something else, they surely weren't really interested in him. Jim's husband had to be extremely persistent before Jim began to believe that his interest was real, personal, and honest. But in the end, Jim's doubts were not really about Addison, or any of those who had reached out to him over the years. Jim's doubts, due to his chronically low self-esteem dating back to those formative adolescent experiences, were centered entirely on himself.

Blaming behavior

Sometimes, low self-esteem masks itself in what appears to be inappropriately elevated self-esteem. That way it is with the person who is never to blame. Whatever the circumstances are, Susan is always right. She doesn't put it that way, but she always seems to find a way to deflect criticism of a mistake or flaw of her own onto someone or something else. Even if Susan and her small son end up running through a torrential downpour to his daycare in the morning, it's always the fault of the weather forecaster who didn't get it right, never her own for not looking out the window and taking an umbrella along. And it certainly never occurs to Susan that she needs to not assign blame in such a case, but should just let it go down as an accident, plain and simple.

In the context of her work, this habit of Susan's makes her colleagues and employees feel belittled, and they view her as overly proud of herself and her own accomplishments. Little do they know that her mask hides very low self-esteem – she blames others because she feels that everyone else always blames her. In reality, she holds herself as a fairly worthless person, and she avoids thinking about this by tallying up the faults of others.

Alternatively, there is the person who always blames himself. Whether the fault is real or imagined, Scott knows deep down that it's his fault. When Scott was nine and his third grade teacher got angry and gave the whole class a lecture on paying attention to the lesson and cleaning up materials at the art table, Scott started to weep silently, because he *knew* she was speaking directly to him! Never mind that he was just about the most attentive student in the class and always cleaned up his art supplies. He was convinced that he must have slipped, and the whole class was getting a lecture as a result. Now that Scott's an adult, he knows a bit better than this, but his first instinct is always to blame himself. Scott's self-esteem must have taken a real beating fairly early in his life to have this habit so well established by age nine.

Risk-averse behavior

Some people are always taking on personal risks, whether it's skydiving or agreeing to a blind date or quitting a bad job before knowing where the next paycheck is coming from. Then there are others who are overqualified for the job that they've held for twenty-six years and would rather not go beyond a ten-mile radius of their birthplace than jump out of an airplane with a parachute.

But what does willingness to take risks have to do with self-esteem? The issue, of course, is one of confidence in one's own abilities. The risk-taker may, of course, be misguided and risk too much, but she suffers from no lack of confidence. Someone who is afraid of taking risks in one or more areas of life probably lacks self-confidence not just in that area, but more broadly. Taking risks implies belief in one's own adaptability, and confidence that one can find a way to get along with a variety of people in a variety of situations.

Nobody loves me, everybody hates me....

One of the surest ways to identify a person with low self-esteem is by noticing a person's feelings that he or she is unloved and unlovable. Such a characteristic shows itself most easily in the personal realm, of course, but even in a business context you can pick out a self-hater. Such a person works alone by preference, eats alone at lunch, and when called upon to work as part of a group, assumes that no one in the group wants her to be part of it. When the team leader proposes to go out for a drink after a hard day's work, our friend begs off. It's not that she has anywhere to go or anything to do, but she's uncomfortable spending time outside of work with people who are surely happy to see the back of her at the end of each day.

In truth, for such a person, living with herself is a task of some difficulty. She doesn't really love herself because if she did she could imagine another person loving her. Instead she ends up alienating others because she presents herself on a social level as something reminiscent of a turtle shell, with the occupant's head and feet drawn tightly inside. This alienation, of course, only feeds the root of the problem – low self-esteem.

Dependence on another's decision-making

It is often easier to sit back and let someone else make a decision. If you've been working hard all day and making a number of tough calls, the last thing you want is to be asked to decide where to go for dinner. However, people with low self-esteem often become dependent on others for decision making, preferring never to be responsible for a final decision. This is the low-level employee who will never be promoted to manager because he always and immediately defers to others in the company. This is the spouse who says he'll have to check with his wife before he can agree to bring a snack to the office party, and who would never dream of going off his list at the grocery store.

What makes a person so unwilling to make a decision? In truth, it's the same issue that's behind so many of these characteristics of low self-esteem – lack of confidence in his abilities in any number of areas, and an inhibited sense of personal responsibility. That may seem harsh, since people with low self-esteem often feel responsible for just about everything that goes wrong, but a life well lived demands a higher form of responsibility – to accept that one is highly qualified to make a decision and that whether good or ill comes from it, it is one's own to make and see through to the end.

Fear of Ridicule

And why does it require fairly high self-esteem to accept such a level of personal responsibility? The answer has to do with a final characteristic of low self-esteem – the fear of being ridiculed by others. "What if the presentation doesn't go well? It was my idea – I just know my co-workers would be laughing at me behind my back." Whether it's a workplace decision or something as simple as a child refusing to wear a certain shirt because her friends will think it's the wrong color, the fear of ridicule stands behind many a display of low self-esteem.

Sociometer theory as well as terror management theory would argue that high self-esteem is strongly linked to group acceptance. It's getting there that is the problem, and finding a way to group acceptance while retaining personal dignity and responsibility.

Looking for the above characteristics is a good way to spot the signs of low self-esteem in self or others; the next step is to find the appropriate tools to reshape those characteristics and raise self-esteem.

HIGH SELF-ESTEEM

Outward Characteristics of High Self-Esteem

Self-esteem is not just a psychological concept used in theories and measurements. It is also a very real life thing that everyone is dealing with at any stage of his or her life. It is related to one's perception of oneself, his or her capacities and traits. It is also one's belief of how others perceive him or her. Self-esteem is a powerful determinant of one's success in all areas of life, including career and relationships with others. Multiple studies show that people with high self-esteem 'attract' success in its variety of forms, while people with low self-esteem do not boast a happy life with many achievements in it. A well-known psychologists Abraham Maslow placed self-esteem on the fourth position in his hierarchy of needs, right after physiological needs, safety, and love. In his view, it is an essential stage to be completed on one's way towards self-actualization.

Psychologists have concluded that the level of self-esteem depends much on a person's early years and relationships with parents in particular. The way how mothers and fathers interact with their children, the way in which they deal with failures and achievements, the extent to which they value the child's opinion and the amount of love and care they are willing to give – they all are crucial for their children's self-esteem. Later, in the years of adolescence, peer groups take parents' place in what concerns shaping of young people's self-esteem. It matters a lot, whether they are accepted or not, respected or bullied, popular or are on their own. Later, when a personality is more or less molded, self-esteem does not change much, but that is only when one does not take action towards modifying it.

In fact, everybody is absolutely capable of improving his or her self-esteem. Moreover, taking care of this on your own and willingly doing so is highly encouraged because it contributes to a person's future successes and achievements, as well as their harmonious relationships with others. Most of all, it gives them an easier view on life which is, in its turn, a key to one's mental and physical health. Below are the outward characteristics and components which together constitute the concept of self-esteem.

Confidence

Being confident is a significant component of self-esteem. A confident person is a person that is well aware of his or her own abilities and powers, and also trusts his or her judgment. It is essential to know how much one can do in order to achieve the established goals, or to just get something one needs on his or her own.

Confidence is mainly the attitude. It is about looking at challenges and seeing that they are manageable, or that they are worth managing in the first place. Those who are not confident will often see obstructions as stop signs, as they will not always believe that they can overcome difficulties due to their perceived lack of personal resources. Still, there are overconfident and pushy people who will go ahead without stopping. Such people are likely to fail, but they are not likely to acknowledge the failure. This is very far from confidence. A confident person would understand not just their capacities, but also their needs. Therefore, it is very important that he or she evaluates the need for achieving an objective before putting any effort in actually doing that.

Aside from acknowledging one's own capacities and being certain of one's own achievement and success, a confident person always accepts a possibility of failure. There is no Superman among us, we are limited in our powers, and we cannot get everything we set our eyes upon. It is a simple truth that a really confident person accepts too.

Self-Direction

You can encounter the concept of self-direction most often in regard to the learning process. If you imagine gaining experience or knowledge as a movement, then self-directed movement would be the one where you are both a guide and director; you define the direction, and you choose the channel.

Basically, self-direction refers to a person's ability to set individual goals and see the way he or she should follow in their pursuit of those goals. Choosing the right course requires a lot of self-awareness. First of all, this concerns personal strengths and limitations. Indeed, when choosing the route, you should take into account all the obstacles and evaluate your chances to overcome them. But in case you cannot do this, why not choose another road?

Secondly, self-direction presumes knowing the goals. To aim oneself in the right course, one needs to know where the stop should be, or at least the pit stop. The goals should be based on individual's own needs and should often serve a bigger picture. For example, a need of finding a job is both a need of having an opportunity to live a self-sufficient life and a need to make a personal input into development of a particular industry. It is not often about the hierarchy of needs, but rather about individual priorities of each and every person.

Non-blaming Behavior

Blame is the enemy of self-esteem; it is something that derives from uncertainty and regret. Regret is what results from over-concentrating on the past. Uncertainty comes out when there is a lack of trust in oneself, lack of ability to either succeed, or recognize this success, or just accept the failure and move on. When a person experiences a fall of some sort, but it is too painful to take responsibility for their own weaknesses or mistakes, blame then enters the picture. It usually spoils everything pretty badly, because it can often be accompanied by other feelings like guilt, anger, or frustration. It surely will not lead one to anything good.

It is always easiest to blame others for our incapability to succeed in something. Finding an external enemy for projecting all bad things on them is, unfortunately, a working solution for many. In reality, blaming others for one's own failures will do no good. At the same time, blaming oneself will do even less. There are lots of more productive ways of dealing with failures and mishaps. For example, a person can think of multiple reasons, for which they did not manage to succeed. Then they can analyze those possible reasons and come up with an improvement plan, so that they can succeed next time. Sometimes, it might just be a mischance; a result of some unfavorable circumstances. It is obvious and natural that there are limitations to one's abilities, as well as things beyond one's control. Accepting this as a part of life is a necessary condition of building up high self-esteem.

An Awareness of Personal Strengths

People are all unique. There is no single individual with the same set of traits, capabilities, and experiences as someone else in the whole world. No two people are similar to that point. Therefore, everyone is good at doing something in particular; those are their strengths. At the same time, a person cannot be keen on doing multiple things at the same time. While there are genii, they are not just rare, but they also have something they are particularly good about and something they are not.

To put it mildly, every person should know their strengths. This will help set goals and then plans for achieving them by choosing the most appropriate routes with the help of the most applicable tools. In other words, it is to know what you want and how to get it. Reaching the desired goal when using one's resources and activating personal capacities contributes greatly to the overall understanding of one's own value and recognition of their ability to function at a higher level. Knowing what you are capable of doing allows you to be more certain in overcoming obstacles, and sometimes even wanting to challenge your personal limits.

You cannot be strong in everything, but only in certain things. You can develop those and be even stronger, or you can work on other abilities of yours as well, so that you can do good in a broader range of things. You also have weaknesses; without recognizing them, you cannot really be regarded as either strong or self-assured person. Besides, all your weaknesses, as well as strengths, single you out from the rest.

An Ability to Make Mistakes and Learn From Them

No one is free from making mistakes, except some ideal error-free robots. In fact, it is even doubtful that the latter exists (or will ever exist). What distinguishes an individual human being from this hypothetical kind of a robot is his or her ability to learn from their mistakes. Mistakes are human, but what is not human is one's demand for their own perfection. In fact, it is little imperfections that make the social world a challenging and endlessly interesting entity to observe and explore.

It basically takes making a mistake, admitting it, making it a part of the individual's experience, and incorporating this experience into further life experiences. It is an endless cycle of learning. So after having incorporated the instance of making a mistake in the overall life experience, a person will make a new mistake at some point when trying new ways of reaching their goals. Although it may sometimes be painful, this is an exciting process indeed.

An Ability to Accept Mistakes from Others

A high demand of oneself is a good thing if those demands are reasonable. In a different case, great expectations might be really harmful. Expecting a lot from oneself can lead to either exhaustion – when a person tries to do more than he or she is capable of and fails after being completely worn out, or result in frustration – when a person understands his or her weaknesses without accepting them. Everyone has the right to make a mistake, and this also concerns people around us.

It is very hard to let go of the mistakes of those who are closest to us, and whose failures affect us in a direct or indirect way. It is important to be able to forgive them, even if they have harmed you without showing yourself as a victim. There are different reasons for people to fail at all sorts of things, but the main reason is that no one is perfect.

Not accepting mistakes from others can be related to blaming them. Neither is consistent with self-esteem, as both are connected in some way with uncertainty. The best way is always to learn from the mistakes; this applied to one's own mistakes as well as to those of others. Not only the person who failed can learn from their negative experience, but you also can as well. In any case, trying to make amends afterwards is often more difficult than forgiving at once. Therefore, trying to get something out of a mishap or error will benefit both of you and, most likely, will even strengthen the bond between the two of you.

Optimism

There was a good old movie, Monty Python's *Life of Brian*. Although it was a comedy, this British film had raised a lot of social and personal issues for the viewer to watch and draw conclusions from. So, at the end of the movie there was a song, "Always Look on the Bright Side of Life." Even as the situation seems inevitable and sincerely bad, it is important that we keep laughing as the titles signal the end of the film. Optimism is an essential component of our ability to turn our weaknesses to our strengths, or to learn from our errors.

Optimistic view on life allows seeing strengths when, at other times, there might be an inevitably gloomy and desperate site. It lets us see the opportunities when, at other times, we see difficulties and obstacles. Courtesy of it, we acknowledge the ups and downs of the world, and, when experiencing a 'down,' we are certain that an 'up' will follow, even though we must make some kind of effort.

Our self-esteem drinks on our optimism and charges with its energy. We tend to value everything better when we see that it's a bit brighter than other things. Thus, when optimism allows us to notice the bright side of ourselves, we perceive ourselves as more worthy of all the good things there are, and we are also more likely to concentrate on our strengths, while treating our minor failures as funny mishaps which could be made into nice little anecdotes.

An Ability to Solve Problems

People's previous experiences play a crucial role in the formation of different mechanisms and abilities, one of which is problem solving. People with high self-esteem find solutions to different problems all the time. Of course, this requires people using their own personal resources, not just material, but also knowledge, experience, their social networks, and so on. Coming up with the best solution presumes that we have evaluated the obstructions, as well as our own powers of dealing with them. This cannot be possible without our confidence and understanding of our own strengths, as well as weaknesses. In the case of the latter, we will most likely try to search for a better way of solving a particular problem. In any case, we can always ask someone for help, which people with high self-esteem do.

Very often, problems or some parts of problems repeat from the previous experience. Thus, it is crucial that a person dealing with problems can apply all the knowledge gained before. It is also important that the current problems are treated as a resource and an opportunity to learn something new (at least, an applicable problem-solving technique).

In general, everyone needs to remember that there is no problem that cannot be solved. It is either personal resources, or others' help which come into action. The 'bright side' approach is surely applicable here as well. Maybe if we look at the bright side, we see the answer that was not noticed when seeing only the dark one.

An Independent and Cooperative Attitude

This is a very tricky characteristic, and an independent and cooperative attitude. It means that both are applicable and in action at the same time. Self-esteem suggests having a positive self-perception, most likely a perception of oneself as deserving respect from others and able to deal and cope with challenges and problems. The latter requires a certain degree of independence.

Firstly, it is independence in making decisions and taking action, and it is also very much about one's own responsibility for these actions. If those were effective decisions, people take pride in making them, and if those were wrong decisions, individuals with high self-esteem do not despair, but accept those decisions and their effects. Secondly, it is one's ability to use their own resources in dealing with different issues without asking for help when it is not necessary.

Nevertheless, it is important that if personal resources are not enough, one asks someone else for help or assistance. There is nothing wrong with that because it just proves one to be human (humans are not all-powerful). Just knowing one's individual limitations and making the right decision based on that knowledge is a characteristic of a mature person, whether they use their own resources or seek for them somewhere else. Cooperativeness is a virtue, and independence is all about responsibility.

Feeling Comfortable With a Wide Range of Emotions

We all like to experience positive emotions and dislike the negative ones. We are all pursuing happiness, and would love to never feel bad or sad. Unfortunately, that is far from possible. An interesting fact is that there are six basic emotions of humans, and only one of them is a positive one, while another is rather neutral. Of the list including anger, fear, disgust, sadness, happiness, and surprise, only the last two can be regarded as positive. We are always comfortable with being happy, but rarely are we comfortable with being angry or sad.

The fact is that all emotions are part of you; they are basic things that, like having strengths and weaknesses, make us human. It is important to understand what you are feeling at a particular moment and not be afraid or uncomfortable experiencing all sorts of emotions. More often than not it is important to communicate your emotions to people around you, but in the mildest way and from your very own point of view. Accepting who you are starts with accepting what you feel, and an emotion is where a person should start from.

An Ability to Trust Others

Trusting no one is a case only when the whole world is against you and when conspiracy theories are true, which means – in popular TV shows. In reality, not trusting others is often equal to not trusting ourselves. Just imagine the world where you cannot rely on anybody, just because you fear that they might turn out to be not trustworthy. Only when you trust people around you can you feel safe and fulfilled, which are the characteristics of high self-esteem.

Trusting others is crucial to the very survival of mankind, as there is usually a consensus between people regarding mutual respect and readiness to provide help when asked for it. Also, even if you think people are not trustworthy in general, your closest circle consists of people whom you chose among the rest; trusting them means better communication and better standing among them.

A Good Sense of Personal Limitations

The ability to feel and understand one's own limitations and the concept of self-esteem are very closely tied. All in all, there is more value not in perfection, but in one's movement towards it. Understanding one's own limitations means that a person has approached those limits of his or her, while exploring his or her own possibilities. This is usually accompanied by setting goals and either achieving them or failing to do so.

Bob Dylan once sang, "There's no success like failure, but failure's no success at all." It is a phrase on which one can think endlessly, but its basic meaning is that success is not possible without the experience of failing, but failing itself is not enough to succeed – one needs to draw conclusions from that experience. So, a person with high self-esteem does not regard the limitations as something completely negative, but rather accepts them and works on building up strengths instead, while growing in directions where they are less restricted.

Good Self-care

As we grow up from helpless babies through adolescents to fully grown people, we learn to take care of ourselves. Although everyone eventually takes care of him or herself, not everybody can boast good self-care. The latter is much related to an image of ourselves that we create and our appreciation of our own selves. The more we recognize our own needs, goals, also our emotions, appearance and personal traits, the more likely we are to tend to ourselves with better acknowledgement.

Good self-care consists of, for example, knowing our own limitations and not trying to exceed them by exhausting ourselves. It can be also something different, such as attendance to our hygiene and appearance. There are lots of ways in which we can take good care of ourselves, by which we will be proving our value both to ourselves and to others around us.

The Ability to Say No

A person who knows his or her own true value will not be doing something that depreciates him or her. Knowing our own needs and tending to them, setting our goals according to those needs and reaching them, doing something we like and enjoying it – these are some of the characteristics of people with high self-esteem. If someone forces us to do something against our will or just asks for a favor that we cannot or have no wish to do, it is the responsibility of ourselves to voice our disagreement by saying "no."

Our ability to say no demonstrates our self-respect towards others, so that they start to respect us in their own way. When saying "no," people filter for themselves, as well as for others, the things that are important from the things that are not. They say "yes" to all that they like, value and need, and "no" to anything that's unnecessary or unpleasant, or for which we just have no time. No matter how much you respect those who ask for a favor, you should remember that you do not owe a "yes" to anyone.

Knowing our needs, we know what is essential for our bodies, souls and overall well-being, and it is important that we have the right to avoid everything else. High self-esteem is greatly constituted by our ability to make our own decisions, take actions based on them and be responsible for our own deeds afterwards. It is always up to ourselves whether to agree on doing something or not. We must always keep our capacities and powers in mind, and also remember about our limitations. Therefore, it is often better to just say "no" rather than to start doing something beyond our capacities, and to allow ourselves to draw the line by saying "no."

LOW SELF-ESTEEM

How Low Self-Esteem Affects Us All

Our world could be said to be infected with an epidemic of low self-esteem. The problem has seeped into virtually all aspects of life, from the way we react and approach life situations to how we consider ourselves.

Whether caused by ourselves or from others around us, when these negative thoughts and influences are at the forefront they have a detrimental effect on how we feel about ourselves and on how we experience life.

Built up over a period of time, this has the power to trigger low self-esteem in us that has a reducing effect on the quality of our lives in a myriad of ways. If this continues without any effort to check it, low self-esteem can even cause issues like depression and anxiety that can lead to serious issues of mental health that can have tragic results.

But what triggers low self-esteem and how does the problem manifest itself in us emotionally?

The causes are varied, but according to clinical psychologists it can often be linked to dysfunction or even abuse in the early years of a person's life. Because it is not possible for us to recognize the effects when we are very young, the negative impact of these early experiences can stay with us well into our adult lives. Some people never ever address them.

Stressful events in our life can also both cause and enhance our feelings of low self-esteem. These could include a breakdown in a significant relationship, financial worries, and low quality care from a parent, career or partner, suffering bullying from a peer, or enduring a relationship that is abusive.

The range of emotions that low esteem encapsulates is many and varied.

Depression: A Dangerous State in Which To Be

Clinicians use a person's low self-esteem as one of the important indicators of depressive disorders.

To disentangle which came first – the depression or the lack of self-esteem – the clinicians use "longitudinal research." This requires people being followed up over a period of time. Findings have indicated almost overwhelmingly that low self-esteem triggers depression but not the other way around.

Therefore, a person with low self-esteem is more at risk of having depression. But, improving that person's self-esteem is highly likely to help the patient feel a whole lot better.

Dr Lars Madsen, an Australian clinical psychologist, says self-esteem is a key factor in both depression's maintenance and initial development. He has identified that sufferers of low self-esteem do not confront their issue to remove it but will attempt to verify it by actively seeking negative feedback. This just further enhances that persons feeling of depression. This has a roller coaster effect because this enhanced feeling of negativity then leads the person with low self-esteem to be seen in a more negative light by others, which in turn leads to more feelings of hurt and rejection.

Being easily hurt

In his book "Born to be Worthless: The Hidden Power of Low Self-Esteem," Dr Kevin Solomon argues that the system of self-esteem we possess can help us to make decisions that are constructive and healthy, but these systems can fail. This failure can lead us to being easily hurt and making choices that harm ourselves and others.

The manifestations can be a toleration of mistreatment, causing ourselves to self-harm, or deliberately hurt others. This could include abusing drugs, sleeping around, eating too much or too little, or harming others by bullying or cheating.

Feeling that we are worthless can have damaging consequences and lead to us feeling angry, frustrated, anxious, ashamed and even guilty.

Anger: Recognize It and Express It

It is normal for each and every one of us to feel anger, but the anger we feel when we suffer from low self-esteem is distorted. When you have a low opinion of yourself, you can believe you are not important to those around you. This feeling of hurt and anger when allowed to build up can lead to furious outbursts.

To try to ensure this does not happen, it is important to teach ourselves strategies for remaining calm. The key to this is learning to express our feelings to those we are with.

If this proves unworkable then the next thing to do is to remove ourselves from the situation that has aroused anger. Take deep breaths – this brings down our heart rate and helps bring us to a relaxed state.

Of course the most important strategy is the one that heads us off before angry situations arise. Often people with low esteem commit themselves to taking on more than they can deal with and then they get frustrated, which turns into anger and rage. We must learn to temper our ambitions and be realistic about our achievable goals.

Frustration: An Essential Part of Life

Unfortunately, frustration is an almost inescapable part of everyone's life. We all suffer those minor irritations – mislaying something, forgetting what we were about to do, getting phone calls when you are up to your neck in other things to do – and all of us have known times when we have failed in what we have set out to achieve.

Because frustration is part of daily life, it is key; we learn to deal with a degree of it so we can remain positive even in the most testing circumstances.

Frustration is caused whenever the goals we expect to achieve do not result from the action and effort we apply. The sources of frustration are both internal and external.

Internal triggers include the disappointment we feel when we can't have what we desire as a result of what we perceive as our own deficiencies, such as shyness or lack of mental or physical fitness. Another internal trigger could be when our goals compete with each other.

External causes can be other people or geography that gets in our way – waiting in queues, listening to recorded messages on the phone saying that "your call is important to us." These things may be unavoidable but we can look for alternative ways to reach where we want to go or choose to call back later. It is important to differentiate between what we can't change and what we can.

Anxiety: A Cornerstone of Esteem

Anxiety is one of low self-esteem's cornerstones.

If our view of our self is less than positive – even negative – then it is highly likely we will approach life with trepidation and go through it full of fear and anxiety.

This can be extreme and permeate everything in a person's life making it almost impossible to make good decisions, sustain ambition, and tackle adversity.

It can sap our energy and fog our minds.

People with low esteem tend to fear anything they believe may confirm their inadequacy. They think others may see they are not up to the task or that they will lose something they have. They fear abandonment, depression, humiliation, or despair.

Shame and Guilt: The Quintessential Emotions

Shame is one of life's quintessential emotions. Complex in form, it is a response we all develop early in life. However, psychologists also see it as the root of dysfunction and as a potential danger if it is allowed to grow unchecked. Shyness, for instance, is one of shame's forms that rarely cause problems — unless it is allowed to become extreme. Humility, another type of shame, is thought to be a desirable social quality.

But there is growing evidence that if shame becomes integral to our image of ourselves it can lead to life threatening problems – including eating disorders, drug abuse, domestic violence, road rage, and all manner of other social concerns.

Whereas guilt can be defined as a feeling of doing something incorrect, shame can be described as the feeling of being wrong. Guilt can be viewed as a positive because it is what tells healthy individuals they have done something wrong. It also helps them change their ways and act responsibly because shame can be seen as unproductive, as it directs people to adopt behaviors that are destructively eroding to their whole sense of self.

Psychologists believe that making their patients aware of their shameful feelings is a crucial step to take in the resolution of this most important psychological problem. Being able to forgive ourselves is a key part of building up our self-esteem. This enables all of us to enjoy our lives and our various relationships.

Guilt and shame may be unrelenting in causing us pain. They may start simmering in our unconscious. This is insidious and can sabotage us in achieving our goals. Resentment, anger and guilt all sap our energies, and keep us locked in the past, preventing any attempts to move ahead.

For those of us who suffer low self-esteem, with issues around shame, it is important to come to terms with it. Beating ourselves up will prolong our shame and guilt, while accepting responsibility improves our self-esteem.

Some suggested steps to improve how you feel about yourself include:

- Take responsibility
- Describe what has happened and how it affected the way you feel.
- Look at what your needs were at the time, and how well they were being met.
- Understand your motives.
- Recognize the catalysts of your behavior.
- Recognize and understand the past.
- Evaluate the standards you use to judge yourself.
- Identify your values and beliefs.
- Understand how your actions affect others.
- Find ways to make amends.
- Learn forgiveness – for yourself as well as others.
- Feel remorse.
- Be honest.

How Low Self-Esteem Affects Us (Thoughts)

Self-esteem can be defined as the impression you have of yourself, based on what you perceive to be your characteristics, strengths and shortcomings. The way a person views himself will determine the types of experiences he will acquire in life, the way he will interact with people he meets and the manner with which he will deal with daily situations. In today's era, there are lots of people who are plagued with low self-esteem due to several reasons. Having low self-worth may be due to incidents occurring during an individual's childhood or events unfolding during a person's adulthood. Examples may be abusive parents, persistent bullying at school, being in a toxic relationship with someone or having financial issues. Low self-esteem can have a huge impact on a person's everyday life and hinder his progress in society. It may lead to missed opportunities, regretful decisions and destructive behaviors. Since the image and opinion a person has about himself will define his level of self-assurance, he should therefore pay attention to each and every thought that crosses his mind. Some of the ways that enable us to identify low self-esteem are listed below:

Negative Self-Critical Thoughts

A human being having negative, self-critical thoughts will possess a bad opinion of his own person and will be prone to chastise himself for every single mistake he does. He will tend to put himself down for every situation that turns out wrong and engage in a damaging behavior by evoking his perceived negative qualities and shortcomings. He will thus actively criticize himself in all dire circumstances for neglecting to meet his own expectations and those of others, feeling that problems arise due to his own fault and he will thus lament on his failings. The situation is analogous to having a personal parrot inside of your head which is always calling you names and constantly putting you down in all situations. Being self-critical will conjure up feelings of worthlessness and disappointment in a person. This will lead to harmful behaviors by causing the individual to withdraw and distance himself from other people, while making him feel guilty and try too hard to atone for things that prompted him to flee from responsibilities and neglect himself. The individual will thus fall into negative emotional states triggered by self-deprecatory thoughts, leading him to experience damaging emotions, like depression and sorrow, which will render him incapable of asserting his opinions and cause him to display passive behaviors.

Unhelpful Thinking habits

The emotional reaction of a person is prompted by the emotional state he is in. The way we interpret situations will determine the kinds of emotions we will be experiencing. Thus, our thoughts are the driving forces behind our responses. These thoughts arise from questions we ask about every situation we experience and the corresponding answer we obtain for the questions. A person with a healthy mind and positive mindset will provide productive answers to the questions, which will allow him to contribute constructively to any situation and give the best of himself in all circumstances. A negative answer, on the other hand, will evoke a plethora of problems which will increase exponentially to support the harmful thoughts and lead an individual to behave in ways that will be detrimental to the situation and to his own self. Thus, the way we think will determine how we respond to all situations. Thus, thinking habits are both helpful and unhelpful, and they determine the behavioral patterns and actions of a person.

Unhelpful thinking habits are consequences of low self-esteem. When a person perpetually doubts his own capabilities and talents, he will think ineffective thoughts and demonstrate unfavorable actions. These thoughts will generate negative emotions like stress, anxiety and depression. Unhelpful thoughts follow a certain pattern which is acquired over time and they can often dictate somebody's behavior even though that person may not consciously be aware of that fact. These thoughts make an individual's life miserable while alienating him from everybody around him.

There are various unhelpful thinking styles. Even though they are undoubtedly related, they elicit dissimilar kinds of emotional reactions from you. It is therefore important for you to identify different thinking patterns and notice how they shape your thoughts and distort your view of reality. A few unhelpful thinking styles are listed below:

Mental Filter

Imagine a sieve in your mind where you can select which thoughts you want to allow through it. Mental filtering, therefore, involves choosing the type of thoughts we want to consider and then discarding those which we deem as not important to us. It is as though you are using a magnifying glass on specific thoughts while ignoring others. A person with low self-esteem will block positive thoughts from developing in his mind and would rather choose to focus on negative ones which will cause him to be in a harmful emotional state. Thus the perception you have of any situation will be flawed as it will be based on a judgment which is tainted with negative emotions.

Mental filtering causes a person to think in terms of problems and then agonizes over them rather than motivating him towards concentrating on finding solutions. It makes the individual focus on only the negative side of any situation and notices insignificant flaws to lament upon. Focusing on negative thoughts will cause him to enter into negative emotional states, like sadness and depression and make him act in a manner that will be damaging to the situation, to other people and himself, first and foremost.

Moreover, mental filtering also involves a person selectively remembering his past. An individual may choose to recall all his negative past experiences if he finds himself in similar situations, instead of choosing to pay attention to how he deals with the present situation. He might also think of past occurrences based on his present negative feelings. A person experiencing pain, for example, might think of a circumstance in the past where he was hurt by somebody.

"Mind reading"

Mind reading consists of assuming that we are aware of what is going on in another person's mind. A person having low self-assurance will invariably think that other people have the worst opinions about him and he will choose to interpret the negative reactions of other people as being in response to his shortcomings and faults. For example, a group of people are angry because they have just been told off for loitering in the streets. The individual with low self-worth, who happens to meet them on the way, might think that they may be angry because of something he has said or done. Another example may be of a partner that is withdrawn and quiet because of the death of a close member of the family. A person with low self-assurance will think that the other person is not communicating because of negative situations occurring between them in the past. Either that or he is trying to distance himself from a break-up or he has met somebody else who is much more interesting and worthy.

Thus, mind reading is not based on facts but rather on speculations on the part of a person who derives his flawed judgments from his own personal thoughts and opinions. It consists of trying to explain someone else's behavior by assuming that we are the trigger for weird or problematic situations. A person with low self-esteem will draw conclusions based on his own insecurities and will feel that he is undeserving of good treatment from other people.

Self-blame

It involves laying blame on yourself for every situation that goes wrong in your life and in the lives of other people as well. Self-blame will cause a person to feel guilty towards situations that are beyond his control. A person with low self-esteem will be prone to blame himself for any misfortune that crosses his way and will make him take responsibility for every single thing that goes wrong. For example, you may choose to lend your car to a friend for a day and it so happens that he meets with an accident.

You blame yourself profusely for being the cause of your friend's accident and creating the situation which led to the harmful outcome. Thus, you fall into negative emotional states by strongly professing your guilt and regret for being the medium of disastrous occurrences.

While taking responsibility is an admirable thing to do, blaming yourself for every single thing that goes wrong in life is self-destructive. Self-blame makes a person miserable and encourages him to wallow in self-pity instead of being rational and thinking that the situation was not in his control. More often than not, a person with low self-worth will choose to be accountable to things that are not his fault at all. Other people's failures and faults are undeniably not your doing and responsibility.

Internal critic

The internal critic resides within an individual's mind and makes general statements about him based on specific situations that occur. For example, you missed the morning bus and reached work late. In a burst of frustration, you exclaim: "I am so incompetent!" Later on during the day, you find out that you have made a mistake in an important report. You again label yourself as being incompetent. A series of events unfold until the evening and you repeatedly tag yourself as being incompetent. At the end of the day, you end up convincing yourself that you are indeed very incompetent and your internal critic is finally satisfied.

A person who adopts such a thinking style will not think in a logical manner, and will analyze each circumstance separately. He will instead choose to distort a situation and make general statements about his behavioral patterns based upon that one incident. In that instance, he will create a poor and false image of himself based on specific mistakes. This has a negative impact on his self-esteem and will cause him to end up making bad choices and failing in other successive tasks. Life is made up of dynamic situations where the same human being placed in similar situations over different periods of time is capable of reacting differently. Therefore, it is wrong to assume that your behavior in a particular circumstance will influence how you behave in all situations in life. A particular occurrence in your life does not determine the outcome of every other situation in your life.

Compare and despair

People engaging in this type of behaviour persistently match their own skills against those of other people and always end up devaluating their own talents in the process. A person indulging in this behaviour will tend to magnify the positive attributes of others, compare those qualities to his own, have a minimalist impression of his own characteristics and thus feel dejected at his lack of skills and talents. The individual will totally ignore his own helpful attributes and will instead focus on those of others. In case he is praised for being successful at something, he will instantly turn it into something negative and affirm that it was only by a mere stroke of luck that success happened or that he managed to do a good thing by mistake. He will refuse to accept something positive out of himself and instead always see himself in a bad light compared to others.

While it is a commendable quality to be humble, the fact of consistently denigrating his own qualities and talents will cause the individual to have low self-worth and hence be depressed in situations that should instead have been uplifting for him. Such kinds of people are unable to accept any favourable outcome out of any situations and in lieu, see positive aspects only in other people while comparing himself negatively against them. A person who thinks negatively about himself will tend to complain about everything in life and be unhappy.

Shoulds and musts

I "should" be able to finish my report by tomorrow morning to make a better impression on my boss, even though a normal person will take three days to finish it. I "must" go to the party this evening on Salina's insistence even though the doctor has advised me to take a week's rest after the accident. Should and must cause you to put unreasonable presumptions on ourselves. You therefore force yourselves to behave in a certain manner based on the high expectations you have of yourselves or the expectations that other people have of you. This puts a lot of pressure on you to achieve what are sometimes unrealistic goals. Such an individual will therefore follow a rigid set of rules that he will impose on himself and on other people in order to meet those goals. He will see to it that he abides by these rules and compel others to so the same while stressing on a defined set of acceptable behavior to him.

Violation of these sets of rules or the display of different behavioral patterns will cause him to become angry and disappointed. He will end up feeling hurt and disheartened when he fails to achieve his impractical objectives. This will lead to feelings of guilt for letting himself and others down. This type of person will be frustrated and will punish himself wrongly for something that was unattainable and unachievable.

Black and white thinking

People who think this way see only the extremes in all circumstances rather than the "shades of grey" in between. They consider people to be either good or bad and situations to be either perfect or disastrous. All people have their good and bad qualities and each situation has its positive side and downfall as well. There is always ground for compromise and mistakes in all situations and people. Reality is never black or white. For example, a person has failed in his final exams. He may have chosen to take exams in five subjects but has failed overall. This does not in any case imply that the person has failed in all five subjects. He may have failed in three subjects and passed in the other two subjects but his overall marks do not add up to the pass mark. Thus, there is always a middle ground where things are neither good nor bad.

People who think in terms of black and white have very low opinions of everybody else and themselves as well while viewing themselves to be absolute failures in case a situation does not go according to their pre-defined way. In such cases, in contrast to trying to steer the situation towards a more positive outcome, they will stagger on the negative aspects and will be determined that there will be an unfavorable outcome for the incident. A person who thinks this way will feel worthless and inefficient, fostering his low self-esteem and causing him to indulge in unproductive actions.

Thus there are several ways in which low self-esteem affects a person in his life. The way you think defines the type of person that you are. As Shannon L. Alder rightly said, "Your perspective on life comes from the cage you were held captive in."

The Effect of Low Self-Esteem on General Welfare

Self-esteem reflects the way we, in general, view ourselves - the general positive or negative emotional estimation of our sense of self, and our self-worth. It covers ingrained beliefs about self, feelings of worthiness, goodness, likeability, etc., and also emotions, such as shame, happiness, or misery; to mention a few. According to Nathaniel Branden, a notable psychologist, self-esteem is the summation of self-confidence (a feeling of personal capacity) and self-respect (a feeling of personal worth).

Low self-esteem, therefore, is the negative emotional estimation of self-worth. A person who suffers from low self-esteem generally tends to see only negative things about himself, believes the worst about himself. When we make room for negative thoughts and pressure to proliferate, either emanating from within ourselves or from external sources, the resultant effect is a low self-esteem that is inimical to the quality of life we enjoy, and with far-reaching consequences on our general well-being. If it is allowed to go on unimpeded, it may lead to mental health breakdown, resulting in problems such as depression. It may even eventually lead to suicide.

Low self-esteem can have several causes, an abusive childhood, or being the product of a dysfunctional family background as a child (which can have a far reaching effect on a person, well into adulthood), or a chronic traumatic experience, such as financial problems, relationship breakdown, bad treatment suffered at the hands of a partner, and many other such situations.

A person who suffers low self-esteem exhibits certain behavioral traits which make him identifiable.

Some of such behaviors are:

People pleasing

A people-pleaser as a general rule, often tries to remake himself into an image that he feels people want him to be, in order to fit in. It generally does not matter to a people pleaser whether the demand made on him and his time is reasonable or not. His all-consuming desire is to be acceptable to the person or people he is trying to please. His own wants and needs are secondary, or irrelevant. His opinions, rights, and desires are also irrelevant. Because a people-pleaser always embraces the ideas and opinions of others, in order to appear acceptable to them, very little is known about who they really are by other people. They never voice an honest opinion about their likes and dislikes. People pleasers will go to extreme lengths, often to their own disadvantage, to please other people. A trait of people pleasers is that as much as possible, they try to appear unobtrusive and self-effacing in a crowd.

Overly defensive of criticism

Low self-esteem sufferers generally feel insufficient in themselves and of themselves; they find it hopelessly easy to think that everyone else sees them in the same way, and that they are the butt of unvoiced jokes. They believe that people will generally reject them, and that no one considers them worthy of respect. They interpret every criticism as a critique of who they are fundamentally, and so they get really defensive when criticism of their actions is voiced because they believe erroneously that all criticisms go to the root of who they really are, and not just a criticism of their actions in a particular situation.

Underachiever and overachiever

People with low self-esteem have a tendency to belong to one or the other of these two categories. They may either be overachievers or underachievers. The former, on the one hand, spends so much time straining to achieve more than is necessary, which they might not have had to if they didn't suffer from low self-esteem. They have an obsessive need to be recognized as a success story, and so give their all and then some to achieving success, in a bid to assure themselves that they are capable. The latter, on the other hand, achieve significantly less than their capacity to achieve might be, as a result of their anxiety and fear of failure or inadequacy, or fear of rejection and being made a fool of. These fears make them recoil from exerting themselves to achieve success, but rather to play it safe and fish in mediocre waters. The overachiever is forever at the mercy of the fear of inadequacy, and as such is trapped in a vicious cycle of pushing himself harder, and becoming a workaholic. The underachiever is no better off because he always has to come up with ingenious ways to ensure that the delicate balance of doing just enough and not a penny worth more is never upset. This puts the underachiever at the bottom of the food chain, with all its associated worries.

Shyness and passivity around people

People with low self-esteem may be non-assertive. A natural reticence is not to be confused with shyness due to a fear of appearing foolish or fear of saying or doing something to upset other people, leaving them open to the consequence of being rejected. They generally refrain from being candid, and would rather make do with what they do not like than ask for what it is they want. They are also never able to be open about their feelings. They generally remain passive, ignoring situations that ought to provoke honest reactions in them, while letting anger and resentment accumulate in their minds, until a minor happening triggers their pent-up feelings, and they react out of proportion to the given situation, becoming acerbic, vitriolic, and in some cases, degenerating into outright violence. People with low self-esteem can also be passive-aggressive, by manipulating situations in a negative way, such as being deliberately late for something important, making snide innuendoes, gossiping, and insidiously causing trouble between persons perceived to be a threat. A person who suffers from low self-esteem may remain passively at a dead-end job and be too afraid to embrace opportunities for advancement, or may remain in an abusive or dysfunctional relationship for the same reason.

Shunning situations and people

Low self-esteem sufferers, due to their self-doubt and being overly critical of themselves, find it hard to form friendly relationships with other people. Considering themselves socially inept, they generally believe that other people will not like them or consider them worthy being friends with. They also have a tendency to avoid situations and circumstances in which they might be criticized, and so they rarely, if ever, venture into new things, particularly when other people are around to see their first efforts. People with low self-esteem generally find it hard to make decisions, due to self-doubt.

Self-neglect and/or abuse

Low self-esteem sufferers may also neglect or abuse themselves. This may take place in many different ways, but it always achieves one underlying purpose: the actions or inactions involved are always to the detriment of the individual's best interest.

A person who suffers from low self-esteem may drift through life taking whatever comes, and generally become underachievers. They never make any significant headway with their lives, and they manage to convince themselves that where they are is the best place that they can manage. Opportunities for self-advancement are shunned out of fear of failing, and they also tend to make the same mistakes repeatedly, never thinking of changing their approach to any given situation.

A self-abuser may also be needy, depending on others for directions with respect to important life decisions. In order to cling to an unhealthy relationship with other people, they may act as if they need assistance, while projecting an image of helplessness. They may also actively court illness or dangerous situations in order to gain and cling to the attention of others.

Another self-abusive habit exhibited by people with low self-esteem is devoting virtually all of their time and energy to work. They concentrate almost exclusively on building a successful career, their own form of self-approbation. This is however a self-abusive trait, because workaholics habitually neglect their personal lives, especially their health and relationships, and suffer dire consequences as a result.

A low self-esteem sufferer may also, as a result of low self-esteem, place so little value on their person that they may become sexually promiscuous, in a futile bid to prove to themselves that they are at least desirable sexually. This anxiety to be deemed desirable is adjudged to be the chief cause of impotence in men, and the failure to reach orgasm in women. It is believed to be generally common in people with low self-esteem.

Lastly, another self-abusive trait exhibited by people with low self-esteem is their desire to test the love of their loved ones by deliberately dropping clues which are clear only to them, but not to other people. They unreasonably expect their loved ones to understand these clues and provide them with what they need. When their clues are not understood or responded to as they expect by their loved ones, they become disappointed and resentful, and also are further convinced of their own low sense of self-worth, saying that if they are worth making an effort over, their loved ones would make an effort to understand their unspoken clues and respond appropriately. In many instances, they jeopardize strong, meaningful relationships in this way.

Physical Effects of Low Self-Esteem

It is no news flash that joie de vivre and a good, positive attitude guard against many ills and promote longevity. A healthy self-esteem is vital for the maintenance of a positive outlook, and overall good psychological health. A low self-esteem, on the other hand, is hazardous to the mental and physical health. As a matter of fact, it is alarming just how many bodily ailments are psychosomatic in nature (a disorder typified by physical symptoms that are the consequences of psychological causes). Whenever a low self-esteem is combined with negative feelings such as depression, stress, and anxiety, it becomes a fatal cocktail in the body that paves the way for illnesses such as heart disease, diabetes, multiple sclerosis and other such dangerous health conditions. A high self-esteem on the contrary fortifies the mental and physical health.

Voltaire once opined that he made the decision to be happy for the rest of his life because it is advantageous to his health. It is a wise decision, because a positive outlook combined with happiness is associated with a high self-esteem, while the negative emotions that usually accompany a low self-esteem gradually erode the immune system and create an enabling environment for different kinds of illnesses, such as heart disease. A low self-esteem amplifies stress. When a person is stressed, hormones such as adrenalin and cortisol are released into the blood stream. Cortisol in particular is associated with diseases such as type II diabetes and hypertension. You can imagine the amount of havoc high levels of this hormone, being steadily pumped into the blood stream on a regular basis, can weak.

Doctors have discovered that people with a family history of low self-esteem and depression are at a high risk for obtaining diseases like heart disease and hypertension. But those who possess healthy self-esteem may actually live their lives without a hint of these diseases to plague their existence. Should they ever find themselves in the throes of such a disease, doctors have noticed that they respond to treatment faster, and are able in some cases be completely healed of the disease, thanks to their mental equilibrium and a healthy dose of optimism.

At this junction, let's examine some of the physical health implications of a low self-esteem:

A weak immune system

The immune system is the line of defense for the delicate organs and systems of which our bodies are composed. It is a highly intricate mechanism and the role it plays in our well-being cannot be over-emphasized. An energetic and balanced immune system is necessary for optimum health. A low self-esteem can do serious damage to the immune system, if unchecked.

People with low self-esteem, because of their brittle mental and psychological state, are generally susceptible to stress. This, if it becomes a chronic condition can affect immune responses. Emotional stress, triggered by feelings of inadequacy, and low sense of self-worth, can trigger depression and anxiety. These negative emotions in turn provoke the release of the 'fight and flight' hormones such as adrenaline and cortisol. Prolonged exposure to these stress-related hormones weakens and eats away at the immune system.

A low self-esteem sufferer, who has a weakened immune system, may find that he is susceptible to the common cold and contract viruses often. He may also be sick a lot, and have allergies. He may also find himself chronically fatigued. All these are symptoms of a weak immune system. The more serious implication is that a weakened immune system leaves you open to grave illnesses like cancer, heart disease, multiple sclerosis, hypertension and type II diabetes; all of which have been said by doctors to be heightened by the presence of cortisol in the system. Various studies have demonstrated conclusively that persons with low self-esteem contract diseases faster than their high esteem counterparts, and also find it more difficult to recover from the effects of even trivial ailments. Another disquieting fact is that expectant mothers with low self-esteem and who as a result have a weakened immune system are more likely to experience stillbirth or have children born with congenital defects, children with stunted intelligence, or children born with the same deficiencies that the mother suffers from, and can also transmit these deficiencies to future generations.

Increase in the levels of inflammation in the body

Inflammation is an important body function. It is the means by which the body fights infections and fix injuries. It is the mechanism by which the body fights all unwanted things, such as germs and toxic chemicals. Inflammation occurs when the body dispatches white blood cells to the site of an injury or infection, and the cells then make available chemicals for your protection. Inflammation can be quite spectacular in its workings.

Ideally, inflammation ought to subside when the immediate problem has been dealt with. However, in certain instances, it may become a continuous thing. One of the factors which trigger chronic inflammation is stress, which is a condition that people with low self-esteem suffer from. When inflammation becomes chronic, it causes serious damage. One of the things which happen during inflammation is that the walls of blood vessels may expand so that more fluids can be secreted into the affected parts. If this happens without check, the tissues of the area of the body where it takes place will remain swollen and hot, and then the blood vessels will degenerate and become congested. Serious diseases such as cancer, heart disease, and arthritis, which are all stress-related, are all aided by chronic inflammation.

Low self-esteem sufferers are run a high risk of chronic inflammation, because they are susceptible to stress, depression and anxiety. If these emotional conditions are allowed to run amok, they may have caused grave diseases like heart disease, and these diseases are accelerated to fatal proportions by inflammation. Even if there are no preexisting health complications, the human body prepares for any perceived threat by boosting its inflammatory response. A person with low self-esteem, who is constantly stressed and anxious, is at risk of suffering from inflammation and the attendant complications of blood vessel damage, and possible organ and tissue damage.

Increase in stress and stress hormones

Low self-esteem and its attendant negative emotions and feelings about self-worth, often triggers stress. When the body is stressed, stress triggers the production of stress hormones, such as cortisol (the primary stress hormone) and adrenaline. Stress is a natural response of the living body to a perceived threat, making use of a mix of nerve and hormonal warning signs. Adrenaline causes an increase in the heart rate, thereby boosting blood pressure and energy supplies. Cortisol acts by increasing blood sugar and enhancing the brains use of glucose, and encouraging the migration of white blood cells to tissues or organs that need repair.

This is all well and good as long as it is done as a response to a legitimate threat. In an individual with low self-esteem; however, stress might be triggered by imagined feelings of being downgraded by other people, or the fear of rejection or ridicule. These negative feelings, though unfounded in reality, may lead to anxiety and stress, and the attendant release of stress hormones, and these hormone levels, rather than abating normally, may continue to rise and stay in the blood stream due to the chronic nature of low self-esteem, for much longer than a legitimate threat might have required. These chronic exposure to stress and stress hormones will eventually lead to a disruption of the normal functioning of the body's processes, putting the low self-esteem sufferer at the risk of a plethora of physical problems such as depression, insomnia, memory loss, weight gain, and digestive problems, to mention a few.

Unhealthy behaviors triggered by low self-esteem

People with low self-esteem as a general rule have a negative self-image. They believe themselves to be unattractive at best and downright repulsive at the worst. They are usually lacking in self-confidence, and spend a great portion of their lives worrying about what other people think about them, usually convinced that it is bad. A low self-esteem sufferer may not necessarily be retiring and withdrawn. They may also be overly aggressive and very competitive, projecting an image of strength while being inwardly plagued by self-doubt and a negative self-image.

Low self-esteem is a key factor in destructive behaviors and getting involved with and staying in dysfunctional relationships. Smoking, excessive drinking, engaging in illicit sex, drug abuse, lack of exercise, eating disorders (anorexia nervosa, bulimia, obesity) insomnia and lack of exercise are some of the harmful behaviors engaged in by people with low self-esteem. Low self-esteem sufferers may have few or no friends at all due to the fear of rejection, and may even prefer to be alone.

Let's take a look at some destructive behaviors exhibited by people with low self-esteem:

Smoking

Various studies have shown, and the World Health Organization concurs, that there is a direct corresponding link between smoking and self-esteem. Low self-esteem rarely begins in adulthood. It starts at the impressionable stages of life, either at childhood or early adulthood. The accompanying destructive behaviors start around that time of life too. Teenagers who smoke do so usually as a coping mechanism for stress and anxiety, and these feelings probably originate out of a lack of self-confidence. Teenagers who smoke usually start as a bid to gain acceptance into a group, and fear of rejection by existing members of the said group who might consider them 'lame' for not being adventurous enough to smoke. They may also smoke to gain the esteem of someone they look up to (a role model), who may constantly put them down and belittle them.

People with low self-esteem may also be secondary smokers, being too passive to either request the smoker to remove from the immediate vicinity, or remove themselves from the vicinity of the primary smoker. They may fear the possible reaction of the smoker and so avoid a potentially unpleasant confrontation by remaining quiet.

In both instances, whether as a primary smoker or a secondary smoker, the person with low self-esteem is likely to ignore the negative health implications of smoking, to the detriment of his overall health, and consequently be exposed to the risk of cancer of the lungs.

Drug abuse

People with low self-esteem try to find relief from the continual mental and psychological buffeting to which they are subjected by seeking relief in some form or the other of escapism. One method of escapism they engage in is drug abuse. They turn to drug abuse in a bid to counteract their insecurity, uncertainty, depression, anxiety and confusion.

Believing themselves to be worthless and deficient in all things, their very existence becomes unbearable grind, and with no reason or motivation to take proper care of themselves, they engage in substance abuse in a futile attempt to escape into an amoral, 'feel-good' world.

The oblivion offered in those few moments of the drug abuse becomes an increasingly attractive option to the drudgery of day to day existence, such that the return to reality and the accompanying problems of going from an extreme high to extreme low becomes increasingly harder to bear, and many intensify the use of drugs with tragic results.

Alcohol abuse

As is the case with the abuse of drugs, a person with low self-esteem, who suffers from a negative self-image, may turn to the bottle in order to find oblivion or a light heart, for a little while. Unfortunately, in the moments of sobriety, which will inevitably come, the low self-esteem sufferer will feel miserable and gauge the reaction of family and loved ones to his lapse into such behavior by his exacting and especially harsh standards of judging himself, which will in turn drive him back to seek escape in alcohol. He is thereby trapped in a vicious cycle of seeking oblivion and the ensuing guilt after the effect of the alcohol wears off. Daily existence becomes a struggle, and the warning signs of health infraction as a result of excessive alcohol intake are largely ignored as he indulges in this destructive behavior.

Poor eating

A little girl of 8 once stopped eating because she was told by an aunt that she was too fat, and fat girls are not popular. The girl's mother had her job cut out for her undoing the damage done to the little girl's psyche by this tactless aunt.

Poor eating habits start in early adolescence, especially among young girls. They are at the stage in life when they believe that the body image is everything. The poor eating habit may be an outright refusal to eat or it could be overeating. A compulsive need to blend in and look like everyone else, while having a negative self-image may trigger a poor eating habit. It has been said that stress can be a cause and an effect of poor eating habits. This is so because a person who suffers from low self-esteem may be stressed into making unwise dietary decisions in a bit to achieve a particular look, often the thin look. On the other hand, a person who is constantly stressed may lose his appetite as a result of the stress and accompanying anxiety, and may suffer stomach ulcers as a result of his lifestyle choices. Poor eating habits may begin as a result of a poor body image, or it may be triggered by other factors relating to self-esteem which have nothing to do with the body image, but with other aspects of the sense of self-worth.

Lack of exercise

Another destructive behavior indulged in by people with low self-esteem in many cases is a lack of exercise. People with low self-esteem in general shun activities that will bring them in contact with other people, or that they feel sets a standard that they must reach, and since they believe so little in themselves, would rather not attempt the activity out of fear of failure.

Exercise causes the release of endorphins, which have been characterized as natural analgesics for the body, helping the body to reduce the perception of pain, and also makes the person feel good about himself. The person with low self-esteem, who is in dire need of positive affirmation, unfortunately misses out on this, as he most probably will not exercise.

An extreme that a person with low self-esteem may swing to with exercise is going from too little to too much. Too much exercise can have a negative impact on the skeletal system and individual may suffer injuries as a result. In this instance also, the low self-esteem sufferer loses out on the benefit of the exercise, because rather than seeing it as the beneficial practice that it is, it has become an avenue for competitiveness.

Eating disorders

People with low self-esteem almost invariably suffer from eating disorders, another destructive habit. Eating disorders are a variety of psychological disorders typified by irregular eating habits, such as overeating or not eating enough. It is an illness that causes serious trouble to the daily diet of its sufferer with accompanying grievous health complications.

Doctors have noted a direct correlation between obesity and depression. Obesity and depression have a common denominator, which is insulin resistance. Insulin resistance obstructs the metabolism of sugar in the diet. The sugar then gets stored as fat in fat cells, leading to obesity, and also because the metabolism is impaired and the end product of ATP cannot be achieved, the resultant effect is that serotonin, a positive neurotransmitter needed to fight depression cannot be produced.

Other form of eating disorders a low self-esteem sufferer may be subject to is Anorexia Nervosa and Bulimia Nervosa. Anorexia occurs when there is extreme food avoidance, to the extent that the sufferer actually starves. It is characterized by excessive weight loss. Bulimia on the other hand is typified by uncontrolled eating and purging. Purging methods may be self-triggered vomiting, the use of laxatives and over-exercising. Those suffering from eating disorders are obsessed with their weight, which is at the root of their negative body image. The weight has nothing to do with whether the individual is fat or thin. The Fat one might be obsessed with the thought of weight loss, but still indulge in excessive eating. The thin person may be so afraid of gaining an ounce of weight that he will be afraid of taking even a mouthful of food, believing deep down inside that the thin physique is the only positive thing he possesses, the only thing that makes him acceptable to people, and so must be protected at all costs, even at the expense of his life, or his health.

Eating disorders are generally accepted to be a problem to which women in particular are susceptible, although it affects men as well.

Low self-esteem is a wide problem. It can affect anyone, cutting across all social, economic and physical strata. A low self-esteem should not be trifled with, and a person who suspects that he might have this problem ought to ascertain whether he does or not by seeking a test to assess his condition. Should you discover that you are indeed in the throes of low self-esteem, get help through either a professional or through any of the self-help websites available online, or join a support group. If all these steps have been taken and you still find the problem firmly entrenched in your mind, then seek the help of a seasoned professional.

WAY OF LIFE TO IMPROVE SELF-ESTEEM

How Do You Feel About You?

Self-Esteem seems to be a hot topic that nobody wants to think about. Sure, one can talk all day about the importance of self-esteem, but do they really apply these thoughts internally? Do you, as a reader, know how you feel about yourself? Assessing one's own self-esteem can be hard. As a species, most of us are prone to looking at ourselves as less favorable than others, and so building it up from there can be difficult. Numerous self-help books have been written on the topic, but we seem to be in the same spot as always.

So how does one first assess their own self-esteem? There are different scales, such as the Rosenberg Self-Esteem Scale and the State Self-Esteem Scale, which will help rate your self-esteem. You can also quickly and simply look at a project you've completed. Were you proud? Were you embarrassed? Did you fall somewhere in the middle? Questions like this throughout the day can help you realize what you think of yourself. When you discover if your feelings toward yourself are generally positive or negative, you can really start working on raising your self-esteem or looking at keeping it at the level it already is at.

Writing is a great tool for raising or at least assessing your self-esteem. Making lists about yourself…your accomplishments, your failures, or just little things you do throughout the day that you feel are of note can help get you to a place where you understand yourself. Focusing on the positives and solving the negatives can create a path for helping you like yourself a little more. As you progress in your writings, you may find that the positives increase and the negatives decrease!

Another way to see how you feel about you, even though it may not be immediately obvious, is to look at how you speak about yourself when people compliment you. Do you argue, or do you say thank you? Accepting compliments is something that many people have a very hard time doing. If you can learn to do so then it can be a huge boost to one's self-worth. Arguing or dismissing the compliment may seem like the humble thing to do, but in fact, you are doing both the person giving the praise and yourself a disservice by projecting to them that their opinion doesn't matter and telling yourself that you are not worth approval. This is what also makes this introspection a valuable tool when looking into how you view yourself and deciding if you need to build your self-esteem.

Looking at yourself with these tricks can help you see where you stand on the topic of self-esteem, and help you to see that you are probably better than you think you are. There are many ways to raise your self-esteem, but the best place to start is in a realistic place and to know how you really feel about you, so that when you're ready to improve, you start from the beginning.

Rosenberg Self-Esteem Scale

The Rosenberg Self-Esteem Scale is a test that can be taken on your own time to help you get a decent idea of how you feel about yourself. The scale was developed by a Sociologist named Dr. Morris Rosenberg and features a series of questions in which you are asked to rate your feelings at the time pertaining to different aspects of yourself. As a tool, this can be immensely helpful in helping one to figure out just how they rank as far as their self-esteem goes. Then when that is figured out, it is easier to start on the path to improvement.

When taking the Rosenberg quiz, you can expect to be greeted with ten questions with a scale of four answers from "Strongly Agree" to "Strongly Disagree." When answering these questions, it's very important to be as honest with yourself as possible because the answer to the test will give you a great starting point in knowing exactly what points you need to work on when going about building your self-esteem.

The scoring on the test is on a scale of 1-4 with a total of 30 possible points, and with a score of 15-25 being considered "normal." Anything below 15 is low. This grading and scaling system is helpful in seeing exactly where the weak points in your self-esteem are. For example, if you score an 8 and look through the test to see that your lowest scores have to do with how other people view you, you could start on your self-esteem constructing journey by learning how to accept compliments, and then make an honest effort to see that the work you do in groups is valuable. If you tend to internalize problems and beat yourself up over them, you could start by making lists of your good qualities. These little exercises are very helpful in building yourself up, and they will help to create an environment where low self-esteem cannot thrive.

The beauty of this test is that in this day and age, tools like this are easily available on the internet and a simple search can bring this test up and open up a whole new understanding of yourself within a few clicks. Having these types of free aids at your fingertips can save a lot of money and time while on the path to self-discovery, and can be a small piece in the puzzle that can bring higher self-worth. A test such as this can be a very valuable aid in the quest for enlightenment, though not the only answer, and by far this is not the only tool. When looking to build self-esteem, the most important thing is to use all tools available, and also to be honest with yourself. It's very hard to admit to low self-esteem, but working through it can make a huge difference in your entire life.

State Self-Esteem Testing

State Self-Esteem testing means that one is being tested on their self-esteem in real time and the state of their emotions at that very time are what are being tested. An example of a test that measures this is the Rosenberg Test, which asked takers to rate their feelings on themselves and how they feel others perceive them at that very moment. Then their self-esteem is measured on a numerical scare, which lets them know how they are feeling about themselves at that very moment.

On the quest to building self-worth, knowing how you feel about yourself at the beginning is a crucial part of knowing how far you need to go. State self-esteem tests go the extra mile because they help you know how you are feeling at that very moment. Nobody feels the same way about themselves all day, every day. We all experience highs, lows, and in-betweens. State self-esteem tests can be taken before work, after work, at home, and out and about, so that you can see exactly how you feel at certain parts of the day while performing certain tasks.

The regular taking of these tests can help you recognize patterns and perhaps adjust your life to try and change these patterns. Say you notice that your self-esteem is higher before work than after work. At first, this could be construed as maybe you had a bad day. If your self-esteem continually drops after a day of work, it might be time to assess if this is the job for you. On the flip side, if your self-esteem is around the same, your job might not be as bad as you think!

After a period of recording and monitoring your scores, the worth building can begin! Record notes of your mood throughout the day as well as test scores. Take notes regarding if your highs and lows come with personal, quiet accomplishments, or with praise, and then try to surround yourself with what helps you like yourself more. Of course, you can't expect praise without giving some in return, so speak to people the way you'd like to be spoken to by people. Praise small achievements, give positive comments, and compliment tiny triumphs, and the positivity will be contagious. You might even find that your self-esteem rises with your increase in positive comments toward others.

In short, state self-esteem tests, such as the Rosenberg Scale, can be a huge gateway to self-improvement with just a few minutes a day of recording your results and trying to spread the positivity to those around you. The important thing to remember is that moods are not static and will change throughout the day, so recognizing patterns can help uncover secrets about what helps you feel better about yourself. Then making changes in those areas can make a huge difference in not only how you feel about yourself, but how you feel about the world around you as well.

BUILDING SELF-ESTEEM

Self-Esteem Development

Self-esteem can be defined as the image a person has of himself. It is a very important factor in determining the kinds of experiences an individual will have in life and his emotional reactions to them. A person with low self-esteem will tend to feel useless and uncared for, while readily blaming himself in all uncomfortable situations and thinking that suffering is his due. He is the one who is actually the source of his own anguish by choosing to listen to his inner critic and wallowing in depressive and negative emotional states. There are various means to help a person build his self-worth.

First and foremost, an individual plagued with low self-esteem should heal himself from within. The person should be conscious of the problem assailing him and accept that he has low self-assurance. This acceptance is the first step towards building his self-esteem. Secondly, he should write down his perceived strengths and weaknesses. Thirdly, he will need to think up situations where he has displayed such qualities and shortcomings, and then analyze his emotional states and behaviors in the respective occurrences. He needs to ponder over the feelings he had experienced in the different circumstances. For example, a person who has made a mistake at work will condemn himself for failing at his tasks and thus undergo negative emotional reactions like guilt, worthlessness and depression. After going through the exercise of introspection, the individual should then imagine himself to be a highly self-assured person or picture a self-confident colleague and reflect on how his alter self or the other person would have reacted in similar situations. Finally, he should ask people closest to him what their perceptions about his qualities and flaws are. This will enable him to understand that what he thinks of himself is a very poor image of who he really is.

Moreover, the person with low self-esteem should learn to silence his inner critic and replace that voice with that of an inner motivational coach. He needs to develop his confidence in expressing himself by initially voicing out his opinions in several situations where he feels he can contribute positively. The individual can also try new experiences regularly in order to boost up his self-image. For example, he may learn to do a creative activity by learning to play a new instrument or decorating cakes. Furthermore, overcoming his fears will also help to increase his sense of self-achievement and self-worth. For example, a person who is afraid to tread in deep waters may persuade himself to conquer his fear and swim beyond the lagoon. New adventures and experiences will enable the person to test his limits and build his self-esteem by being successful in overcoming the barriers in his mind, which hindered him from leading a positive life.

The Real You vs The False You

What define you are your thoughts, personality and character. However, what is apparent is your emotional reaction that is conveyed by the things you say and do. Often times, several factors hinder a person from being true to his own self. A person with low self-esteem will repress his opinions and talents by persistently lauding his faults due to his inner critic and wallowing in misery. A person's thought processes will determine his ensuing emotional states and reactions. There are several factors which cause a person to display behaviors and attitudes which are contrary to his own personality.

Peer pressure is a blatant case where a person reveals a false version of himself. For instance, an individual may feel coerced into smoking for the sole reason of not being alienated from his peers, who are people that find smoking to be a 'cool' activity. In this case, the person goes against his own will and thoughts in order to act in a manner that does not reflect his wishes. Thus, the person chooses to yield to emulating the action of his peers. Another example may be of a person who tries to copy the style, look and interests of another person who is very popular and self-confident. The individual with low self-worth will aspire to be in the place of that other person and think that it is achievable by imitating. In doing so, the person loses his individuality by trying to be like someone else as well as his own identity and personality. Therefore he projects a false image of himself and is determined towards achieving that illusion.

Learning to develop self-esteem allows a person to shun the cover that is masking his real self and to let go of the fake image he has of himself. In doing so, the person will stand true to his own identity and be able to speak his mind in all situations instead of going with the flow. Increased self-assurance allows a person to be transparent and honest in his actions and behaviors, while affirming that he is truly unique in his own way. It also enables an individual to be confident enough to follow his own aspirations and dreams instead of being tied down by the visions of other people. Thus a person should be able to be himself in all situations and not let himself be dictated by other people on how he should think, act and react.

Moreover, people should not adopt a perfectionist attitude. Human beings are liable to error and if somebody has such an attitude, he will always be blaming himself for failing to meet his expectations. A person with high self-esteem understands that all situations in life do not go according to their wishes, so they are able to accept their vulnerabilities and weaknesses.

Read/Watch Inspirational Stories

A person having low self-esteem will invariably linger in a vicious circle of negative emotions while shying away from opportunities that life presents to him. In this sense, inspirational stories and movies can serve to alter the negative emotional state of a person and cause him to question his life, attitudes and behaviors. Some stories and films are based on the true life events of other people who have managed to overcome their phase of low self-worth and developed their inner motivation in order to achieve their goals in life.

The Alchemist, written by Paulo Coelho, elaborates about a shepherd in Andalusia who dreamt about a treasure found in Egypt and the path he takes in order to fulfill his dream. The novel is an inspiration to many people around the world and it stresses about the importance of taking the leap of faith required to achieve one's dream. The shepherd makes a series of decisions which brings him closer to his goals, and the choices he makes transform his life totally. The writer carefully illustrates the internal conflicts that the protagonist goes through and how he overcomes each situation successfully. The Power of Now by Eckhart Tolle deals with the importance of focusing on the present moment instead of lingering on past or future events. It evokes the fact that past and future moments are only occurring in a person's thoughts while he is living the present moment. It also suggests meditation and relaxation techniques to let go of anxiety and worry. The monk who sold his Ferrari, by Robin Sharma, is another inspirational book that narrates a story about a successful lawyer who gives up his fame and money in order to embark on a journey in search of himself. The book is basically about self-discovery, finding out who you really are within and what meaning you want to give to your life.

The secret, by Rhonda Byrne, is a novel which has been turned into a short movie and it explores the law of attraction. It basically discusses about the way our thoughts influence different events occurring throughout our lives. Positive thoughts attract favorable occasions while negative thoughts will lead to harmful happenings, hence the law of attraction. If you focus on things or events that you fear and hate, they will eventually manifest themselves in your lives. The Bucket List is a movie concerning two terminally ill men who set out on a journey to complete a list of things they wish to do before they die. The story underlines positive living, enjoying the present moment, the ephemeral nature of life and the way you should go about by making your life worth living and creating memories worth remembering. There are many such inspirational movies which accentuate the importance of having a positive attitude towards life. TED videos constitute a series of genuine motivational stories about people who have managed to overcome their low self-esteem in life.

Control your emotion

Emotional Intelligence is an important aspect in determining the way a person lives their life. It defines the level of self-confidence a person possesses, which will enable him to tackle day-to-day problems. According to Daniel Goleman's Five Pillars of Emotional Intelligence, self-awareness is a prerequisite in order for a person to have high self-esteem. It consists of being aware of your emotional states and the effects they have on other people. A person should be able to identify, analyze and understand his own emotions and impulses. How a person reacts to a particular situation depends on his level of awareness of the emotion he is experiencing and his ability to control it. Another component of Emotional Intelligence is self-regulation, which is the ability of an individual to control his emotions, curb his negative impulsive responses and to think before expressing his emotions.

A person should thus learn to suspend judgment in any particular situation and think carefully before acting. For example, in a situation where an individual gets depressed because of the words uttered by someone else, the person should first be conscious that he is experiencing depression. He should then question the reason why he is in such a damaging emotional state. The next step would be to analyze his impulses and reflect upon whether his emotional reactions will be constructive or destructive. Despair is a very harmful emotion. The person needs to learn to detach himself from situations that have a negative impact on his emotional state and then develop his logical thinking skills. The individual who involves himself emotionally in all situations will tend to have extreme emotional responses. The one with low self-esteem will agonize upon his fate and refuse to be impartial towards circumstances in his life. Therefore, a human being should not let a situation or another person alter his emotional state and elicit negative reactions from him.

Moreover, a person should practice controlling his emotions. For somebody accustomed to resorting to destructive emotional states and behaviors, it will be a challenge to change their thought processes and foster positive thoughts and emotions. For example, if an individual experiences negative feelings, like guilt or anxiety, they should first think in a rational way and view the situation objectively. Only after carefully examining the circumstances can they then give their judgment and decision. Furthermore, empathy is another component of emotional intelligence. A person needs to understand the emotional setup of different people and treat those people according to their emotional reactions. In doing so, an individual can easily read another person's emotional state and avoid being emotionally engaged in the situation.

People who are emotionally intelligent have a better attitude and outlook on life. They perform well at their jobs and respond better to challenging situations.

Liberation from Guilt

Guilt is an emotion that eats at a person from the inside and causes the latter to engage in harmful behaviors. The individual who is feeling guilty will try and make it up to other people in order to salvage the situation in any possible way, while invariably blaming themselves for failing to meet their own expectations as well as the expectations of other people. For example, in case a person makes a mistake at work, they will blame themselves for failing at their duties while ignoring the other factors outside of their control, which has led to the situation at hand. Feelings of guilt are deeply entrenched in a human being's childhood through the way they were brought up. Parents usually rebuke their children for specific behaviors while congratulating them when they display other types of reactions. A child needs to be made aware of the reasons why certain conducts are encouraged and others are discouraged. Parents utilize punishment as a means to elicit feelings of guilt from their child in a way that if the child finds themselves in similar circumstances, they will feel guilty without really understanding why they are going through such emotions. This childhood indoctrination is deeply embedded into your nervous system and you take such memories with you into adulthood as well.

Guilt is beneficial to people only in small doses and should otherwise be transformed into love and positive emotions. Liberation from guilt is a long process for those who persistently suffer from the sentiment as it consists of reprogramming our nervous system and changing our perception of life. A person should learn not to let incidents that occurred during their childhood to influence them. For example, a parent can continuously say to their child that the latter is useless and the cause of misery and worry for everybody. The child grows up believing that indeed all bad situations happening in their life are because of them and so they end up blaming themselves and feeling worthless throughout their life. This majorly impedes their progress later on in life and they are unwilling to take any initiative in order to improve their situation.

The most advisable thing to do is to distance yourself from people who manipulate circumstances and your emotions to make you feel guilty. People who bring out such feelings from others are a poison to healthy living. An individual should learn how to analyze their feelings when they find themselves in such emotional states and should be able to identify their triggers for guilt. Thus, they will be able to better control their feelings while not letting them become overwhelming. In doing so, it will be easier for them to explore the incidents in his past which have elicited emotions of guilt from them. In recalling these occurrences, they can better judge the situation with another perspective and way of thinking. Music has also proved to be very useful in driving away negative sentiments of guilt.

Conquering Your Inner Critic

Everyone has a critic living inside of them. This is the voice that tells you that the job you did might not have been so great after all, and that you don't look very good or shouldn't feel good about yourself. Some let the voice get too strong, and this can quickly wreck your self-esteem. It is normal to have some spells that are worse than others, but when your critic becomes the predominant voice in your head then it's time to learn how to conquer it.

The first step is realizing what your points of insecurity are. Journaling can help you to pinpoint these aspects, as can gauging your mood at certain points during the day using useful scales such as the Rosenberg Self-Esteem Scale. Checking your self-esteem before a project and then again after can help you see if your work is bringing you down, or maybe your self-esteem grows after completing a household chore. Recognizing these patterns is a very important first step to owning and controlling your inner critic.

The next step is learning how to accept that you do have flaws, and learning how to not hang onto failures or dwell too long on the negatives. This sounds easy in practice, but as everyone knows, it is actually very difficult. What you may find helping is interrupting the thoughts before they become persistent. Have a list ready of things you are proud of, especially things that are pertinent to the situation and that can help you when the doubts start creeping in. If you feel as though you're about to start criticizing yourself, think of the items on your list that make you proud and focus on that until the doubts start to subside.

A final step in beginning to conquer your inner critic happens when the first 2 steps are performed consistently. This step comes after the first two become a habit, and it is more of a change in your way of thinking. After applying the first two steps, the final step sort of completes itself because you will naturally start to find the positive in what you've accomplished and downplay what you formerly saw as flaws. You'll find that the more you consciously review and assess your feelings, the more control you'll have over them. Knowing what makes you react negatively to a situation helps you realize what you need to do to avoid or fix the feelings quickly rather than dwelling on them, which is so common.

Overall, you inner critic is a stubborn nemesis that can be overcome with repetitive training to learn how to calm and quell the nagging that many of us are so used to. Exercises, such as the ones listed above, can help quiet the critic as well as increase your self-understanding in many different ways. The exercises can help you become a better rounded person and will definitely help in your everyday battle with your critic.

How to Leave Insecurity Behind

Insecurity is a feeling that plagues most people, yet it is something that is very difficult to discuss with our peers. Everyone wants to appear like they have it all "together" in front of their coworkers, and usually are unwilling to want something as seemingly "weak" as personal insecurities out in the open in front of even our closest friends and family. We will explore learning how to leave the insecurity with insecurity behind, and see how important it is to build yourself up and also learn how to open up to more people and be able to share insecurities. You might be surprised that they share some of the same ones and you may be able to help each other find different ways to overcome them.

When looking to leave your insecurity behind, you must first realize what is causing it in the first place. Is it work related? Relationship related? Does it have to do with your looks? Journaling is a great way to gain some introspective on your feelings and how your mind works because sometimes we get so caught up in our own little routines of feelings that we forget to really process how we're feeling and why. Writing it down as it happens or soon after can help us realize things that may not have been immediately at the surface and can help along the road of overcoming insecurities.

As stated above, confiding in people you trust can also be a huge help in overcoming your insecurities. It is hard to admit when you feel as though you aren't adequate, but having a friend or family member that can help lift you up is one of the most helpful things you can do for yourself. Be open about what you want to talk about, and let them know that you are there for them as well, and a very intimate and fulfilling relationship can form as well as a valuable resource in fighting your insecurities.

You don't have to depend on someone else for these things either. You can be your own best cheerleader. In order to do this, it is very important to realize what upsets you and what lessens your stress. When you feel yourself becoming insecure, remember something that you were proud of yourself for and then conjure that up before you allow yourself to continue down the cycle of insecurity. Have a list of things ready that you know you did well at, and make sure you engulf yourself in them when you feel your mood about to go downhill.

The road to overcoming insecurity is not an easy one, but it can be done with self-awareness and a good support system. Remember that you can also be a good support system for yourself. Don't forget to give yourself praise on things that you know you deserve praise for, and know that you are not alone!

Pursuing Happiness and Finding Your Joy

What makes you happy? When asked this question, most people can come up with a pretty standard list, "Friends, family, reading, hiking…" but how many people talk about what little day-to-day things bring them joy? What can you do in your life to make sure that every day brings happiness?

Everyone has several "big" activities that make them happy. You can ask anyone and they'll most likely have something that is an all-encompassing activity to share, such as museums or art. What many people don't realize is that they can find little pieces of happiness throughout their day and that can lead to an overall joy when combined with their bigger happy activities and other smaller joys.

A great way to find what makes you have a smaller happiness; journaling is something that may bring to light some little activities that get you through the day as well as help you realize things that you never knew made you happy. For example, a cup of tea after a long day at work, followed by a favorite TV show and even some journaling, can add so much to your life.

Looking at what brings you joy may bring some unexpected revelations. Maybe you've always found solace in folding laundry or dusting. Maybe you enjoy cooking an extravagant dinner. When looking to find your joy, look to activities that you do when you want to lessen your stress to unwind during the day. After that, you can take notes and see what little things you do that might not immediately come to the forefront of your mind.

Ultimately, when it comes to finding your happiness and realizing your joy, it comes down to knowing what makes you happy on a larger scale as well as the little things that you can do to help get you through the day on a positive note. This is because the larger happiness is due to the strength of the character, but the essence of true joy lies within the most secret part of a person.

Unleashing this secret part requires a bit of intimacy and practicality. Make a list of the little things that make you glad during the day, or things that release you from stress…that will help you realize that the second cup of coffee is giving you a huge boost during your day. Not of energy, but of happiness. Little things like this will help you understand what you truly feel as happiness in your life.

It is so important to give equal weight to the little things in life rather than just the major things that the media focuses on. Joy can be found just as easily in a book as it can in world travel. Remember to give equal strength to the little joys, such as a new decoration, as you would give to a new job. The extra joy will radiate through all of the work you complete and inspire new creativity.

Learning How to Love Yourself

When asked how they feel about themselves, most people choose to answer via the modest route, and say something along the lines of, "Oh, I don't know…I'm okay." When asked to truly review how people feel about themselves, the results don't differ much from how it was brought up in a casual conversation. Frankly, in our culture we are taught that loving yourself is selfish, and not a positive trait at all. This leads to many people not wanting to vocalize love for themselves, and as a result, the feeling gets internalized.

Loving yourself doesn't mean that you aren't a humble, caring human being, and it certainly doesn't make you vain or selfish. In fact, learning how to care for yourself can help you love others even more, as taking a little time here and there to nurture your body and soul relieves stress and can create an environment where you are able to actually love people more, since you are in a better state of mind.

How does one go about learning to love themselves? It is something that takes time and patience, as all of the years of learning to put a backseat to yourself are difficult to undo. One of the first and best steps is journaling. Keeping a written record of your thoughts and actions over a day can help you learn more about yourself, and thus give you more to appreciate. Listing qualities you like and thinking about them when you are down can also be helpful.

Something else that is so very important, but also incredibly hard is learning how to give yourself the time to do things strictly for you. This is what a lot of people really struggle with because they view that doing something for you and you alone is selfish and counter-productive. How are you supposed to get anything done if you stop and take a moment for yourself? However, just stopping to enjoy a chapter of a book while sipping some tea, or doing some stretches, or even splurging on a massage every now and then can make you more productive because you won't be as bogged down by negativity. Taking the time to do one little thing for yourself a day is also a great way to show yourself that you like yourself, and starting small will eventually lead to bigger treats that grow easier to accept with time.

Learning to love yourself isn't easy, but with time, patience, and the willingness to let yourself take a little extra time each day to relax or do something that is just for you, it can be done. The hardest part is remembering that, rather than being selfish, these things help us be better for everyone around us as well.

Developing Your Character and Spirituality

Character and spirituality are very personal traits that many people hold close to their hearts and keep private. Deciding how you want to be seen and what your beliefs are can be a very long road, but very rewarding when you decide that you want to go about developing these characteristics. Having personal beliefs in the spiritual or even the non-spiritual form can help define you as a person and shape your personal character as well.

First, character is a multi-faceted term that describes how you are on the inside, but also how people perceive you. Your character may be described as altruistic or greedy, good or bad, and sometimes what we project onto others isn't exactly what we feel on the inside, and some things may be perceived one way, but actually have ulterior motives. Understanding your character and developing into what you want to be is a very important step in becoming the person that you want to be remembered as.

Spirituality is the belief in something that is not of this world. Obviously, this differs all over the Earth and even very greatly from person to person. Often a person's spirituality dictates at least certain aspects of their character. Some may belief in not eating pork, and some may not engage in relations outside of wedlock. These beliefs stem from a certain set of traits that the their own form of spirituality holds in high regard, and so people strive to become that ideal and this is frequently done in a church or temple setting, where people can be around other like-minded people and see how they measure up or what they can do to help themselves become this ideal.

Of course, not all spirituality has to be in the form of group worship. Everyone holds onto their own set of beliefs, and then acts accordingly. The vast array of religions and sects means that there is room for interpretation, even within a group that on the surface shares beliefs. It seems that the strongest relationships form out of personal and private interactions with their beliefs.

To develop your own personal spirituality and character, it is a good idea to look at what you really believe. Try a lot of research and try out a lot of places. Think of who you want to be as a person and research which group of people most closely matches that. Most importantly, spend time reflecting with yourself and seeing what is best for you. Do you prefer the support of many others or the quiet solitude of meditation and reading by yourself? The ability to know yourself and what fits you will be a huge help in your path toward spiritual development.

The Power of Beliefs

Beliefs are a very powerful and personal matter that many people have, but not many people talk about. Having a set of beliefs is something that connects most people all over the world. Even though everyone believes something different, most have something they believe in and it shapes them as a person. Beliefs can dictate character, actions, and feelings, so they are a very influential presence in people's lives.

By having a set of beliefs, you are subscribing to the nature of those beliefs, and therefore, on some level, choosing to live your life by them. Allowing yourself to become connected with powers beyond what you can see can open up a lot of doors in your life, and help you to gain peace and relieve stress. It also serves to provide social wellness in certain settings, and can untie people that may never have met.

How you connect to your beliefs is up to you, but many people find prayers, churches, temples, or meditating to be ways of bonding with their deity or other spiritual guide. These practices also force you to center yourself and relieve yourself of some of your worldly stresses so you can focus on what you want to become spiritually and allow their to be a huge calming influence in having beliefs.

Beliefs also have power in that they can help bond you to other people who share similar thoughts on the universe. These relationships can be made to be very strong since you spend time talking about troubles, blessings, and other life events that come along and affect you and strengthen or weaken your beliefs. Keeping friendships that help to build and sanctify your beliefs and in which you do the same also helps you learn empathy, which is a wonderful feeling to master.

Subscribing to a set of principles and philosophies is a great way to find comfort in difficult times, as most sets of beliefs are able to give advice in their holy texts, scriptures, or guide for living that will help calm the nerves, ease the grieving, or show a path to joy. The security that comes with knowing these texts or guidelines, and knowing that they've helped many people before you is a great help in times of strife, and another example of how beliefs hold power.

The world can be so diverse, but yet most cultures hold onto similar beliefs. This is an amazing thing and it shows that no matter what your particular set of beliefs are, the need to have something to worship, study, and bring comfort to us is almost universal, and that can also bring us together. The power of beliefs is in the fact that huge communities can believe one thing, yet also have diverse personal beliefs. But overall the object is to comfort and promote mental well-being by giving people a guide for living their lives.

Looking to the Future

In today's world, there is an ever-present need to be in the now. With smart phones, e-mail, work, and family, it has become harder to plan for the future, much less think about where you will be in 5, 10, or 20 years. This can put a strain on things, as money can be hard to put away for later, and with fewer people having long-term careers at the same company, it is much more difficult than it used to be for people to project what will become of them.

When looking to the future, it is a good idea to look at several different aspects: money, career, entertainment, and housing among many others. Where will you get your money, where will you work and live, and what will you do? What do you want out of yourself and your life and how can you achieve it?

Deciding what you want for dinner is hard enough, but deciding how you want to move forward with life is even more challenging. When looking to the future and trying to figure out what you'd like out of life, a journal or just a few moments making lists based on wants, needs, and devices you can use to get there can help tremendously. Start by making a list of what you enjoy doing. If you feel you are in a dead-end job, you can make a list of what makes you happy, and then brainstorm careers that have these traits. You can then make your present about working toward the goals of what you want to do with your future career.

If you want to live somewhere else, start making lists of what you can do to accomplish moving there. How much money you'll have to save, where you can look for a job, and what neighborhoods strike your fancy. Look into schools if you have kids, and see what activities are big in the area.

Preparing for the future can be a daunting task, but it is one that is well worth it, and by formulating a plan and thinking about it ahead of time, you can make the later changes you'll have to make just a little easier because you will not be thrust into them, but rather have a path paved for exactly what you want to be doing.

Of course, life throws us all curveballs and not everything will go according to plan, but having at least the larger pieces figured out will make any transition much smoother. Even when little things don't go right, the bigger picture can remain intact. Sometimes the biggest goals look smaller and less daunting when broken down on paper, and you'll be surprised at what you can achieve by looking toward the future.

You Can Change

It seems like the older we get, the harder it is to change because we get so set in our ways and stuck in routines that may or may not be beneficial to us. Often, we don't change because we don't know quite how to go about it. This is a self-fulfilling trap that many of us get stuck in, and we just continue to live the lives that we've been living for years.

The first step in changing is figuring out what you want to change. Do you want to switch careers? Move? Lose 40 pounds? Depending on what you want to do, the steps on the way to succeeding will be quite different, but fulfilling these can start out very similar even if the end goals are so different.

First, you must examine what you want to change. This can be harder than it sounds. You might have a vague idea of what you want, but have no idea of what the final version will look like, and the path to achieving that goal can seem even vaguer. Journaling what you like, want, and hope for can help.

Even more than journaling, creating lists with very small and achievable steps can be used as powerful tools for laying out your path to change. For example, if you wish to lose weight then you can first think of your end goal, and then write out steps to achieve it. The trick is making the steps as small as possible so that you can see that you are progressing on your path to change. Instead of just saying "exercise," say "20 push-ups on Monday and 25 on Tuesday"...etc. This is much less daunting than just simply ordering yourself to do it, and therefore, will usually show more success.

Next, recognize the small changes that you notice to keep yourself from giving up. If your goal is to change careers, recognize yourself for getting an interview in the field instead of beating yourself up if you don't get the first job you interview for. This is very important for keeping your self-esteem up and to keep you going on the path of meeting your goals and changing.

Finally, become the change you want to be, or fake it until you make it. It's emotionally hard to change, and there are bound to be failures along the way that can make you want to give up. It's an unfortunate fact of life. However, if you tell yourself that you're going to keep trying after a setback and adjust your plans accordingly, you are more likely to stay on track. Remember your goals and that small step are a great way to stay on track, even in times of strife.

Practice, Practice, Practice

When looking to change your life and become the person you want to be, there is nothing like practice. Many people associate practice with just sports or children learning their multiplication tables, but practice applies to every aspect in life and can be invaluable in becoming who you want to be or changing any aspect of your life. Nobody can change overnight and practice can be applied to every aspect of life to help you become the best version of yourself.

Practice doesn't have to be a person just repeating the same action over and over again; it can happen on paper or while playing out scenarios in your head. Lists and realizing what path one needs to follow are good ways to induce practice in your head, and think ahead to what you'll do during any sort of situation. Living through situations before they happen can be great social practice and will help you be able to think on your feet a little bit better so that you don't freeze in critical life situations.

Preparedness can be seen as a huge form of practice. Writing out what you want and figuring out the best way to accomplish things is also a very good way to practice, since you can't very well physically practice the steps day after day. The writing and planning will make it seem like you have practiced in person though, as you will be prepared for many scenarios because you thought them through ahead of time. Dry runs can happen with drills if the provisions are available, or even something as simple as holding a conversation with yourself in the mirror can be helpful forms of preparing and practicing for many different situations.

When you get into the habit of practicing every day, you'll be surprised at how it leaks into other aspects of your life and helps you. Knowing that quickly going over something in your head and playing out different outcomes can help prepare you for so many different social interactions and then people will notice that you are more comfortable and confident.

Of course, sometimes practice is physical rather than mental. If you want to be a knitter, you'll knit until it becomes second nature, and that's the entire purpose of practicing both mentally and physically; to turn certain actions into muscle memory. The more you perform a task, the more naturally it comes the next time and therefore, the more of an expert you become. Practice really does eventually make perfect in all aspects of life. Making sure you know what you want and then dedicating time to practice, practice, and practice is the most important step in becoming an expert in whatever you'd like to be an expert in.

Using Affirmations to Change Your Thinking

Reprogramming negative thinking can be difficult, but there are ways to help you do so. One of those ways is through using affirmations.

What are affirmations? Webster's Dictionary defines an affirmation as "a statement asserting the existence or the truth of something." In other words, an affirmation is a statement saying "this exists" or "this is true."

Positive affirmations are positive words and thoughts that program your mind, similar to the way a computer is programmed. They help you focus on your goals, or your desires. Affirmations create mental pictures in your conscious mind. The mental pictures in your conscious mind then affect the way your subconscious mind works.

It's best and most effective to write affirmations in the present tense. Why, you may ask? Your subconscious mind takes certain things very literally. If you're using an affirmation such as, "I will (lose weight, begin to exercise, etc.)," the subconscious mind may interpret that as, "I'm going to do this someday in the future." The subconscious mind then keeps it as a future goal, not a present goal. In writing and using affirmations, you give your brain a specific direction to move.

Here are a few steps to take when creating affirmations:

1. Get alone and find a quiet place where you can think and focus on what you want to achieve.

2. Answer the question, "what do you want?" and make the answer as specific as possible. (For example, "I want to lose 20 pounds," rather than, "I want to lose weight.")
3. Create a mental picture of the change you want. Visualize a thinner version of you or see yourself running a 6K.
4. Get a pencil or pen, and write down the goal you are thinking about.
5. Write your affirmation underneath the goal. Make it personal
6. By starting with words such as "I am. . ."
7. If you choose to, include a present tense verb, such as "I show," "I respond," or others.
8. You can also add a positive emotion to the affirmation. "I am excited about . . ." for example.
9. Finish the affirmation with the results you want. "I am excited about the relaxed person I am becoming."

Repeat the affirmation at least twice a day.

Here are a few examples of positive affirmations:

- I accept myself.
- I believe in myself.
- I am excited about my healthy weight of 165 lbs.
- I have confidence in myself.
- I am a skilled communicator.

How long does it take for affirmations to work? Reprogramming your brain out of negative thinking takes time. And the specific result you are looking for from an affirmation (such as losing weight) also takes time. But your mental reprogramming can begin immediately when you start using affirmations. Your job is to create an environment for them to flourish.

You can choose the way you think. Affirmations are a way to help you reprogram your thinking. Try it. You only have your negativity to lose.

Strengths and Weaknesses: Figuring Them Out

Strengths

- "So, what do you consider your strengths and weaknesses?" This question is a common one in interviews. It's also a good question to ask yourself when it comes to other personal goals.
- We all have strengths, and we all have weaknesses. In order to know yourself, you need to know what your strengths and your weaknesses are.
- What are "strengths?" Strengths are things that come naturally to you, the abilities and desires that "click." Think about the question, "If I didn't have to worry about money, I would do . . ."
- Or perhaps, you've been doing something . . . and then, you glance at the clock and think, "Wow! Where did the time go?"
- What were you doing then?

The answer to those questions may reveal a strength you have.

Weaknesses

Weaknesses, on the other hand, are things about yourself where you can see room for improvement. At times, "room for improvement" means learning some "life lessons" (like, how not to be consistently late). Other times, "room for improvement" can mean trying to master certain necessary skills.

So how do you determine what your strengths and weaknesses are? How do you know what you're weak in and what you're strong in?

Here are some ideas:

- What is it that you really like to do? What sparks your interest? What sets you "on fire," so to speak? These may be signs of strengths.
- What do you tend to avoid? What are things that you do but it seems like treading water or slugging through mud to get through them? These may be signs of weaknesses.
- Ask people who know you: "What do you consider to be my strengths? What do you consider to be my weaknesses?" An outside viewpoint may help you in realizing areas you're strong in that you may not be aware of.
- There are aptitudes, personality, and other such tests that can help you get a handle on what your strengths are. These are usually administered by professional counselors and psychologists. One example is the Myers-Briggs Type Indicator, which shows personality differences amongst sixteen personality "types."

Once you know your strengths and weaknesses, you can act to maximize strengths and work on weaknesses. Some people prefer to focus on their strengths. For example, if you're a right-handed baseball player, it wouldn't make sense to try working on being a left-handed one. Rather, it would be better to keep focusing on your strength of being right-handed.

On the other hand, if you desire to work on a weakness, here are some suggestions:

- Enroll in a class or join an activity that may address your weakness, such as a public speaking class for those afraid of speaking in public.
- Find support, such as a group of friends, or even professional help, like a therapist.

If you want to know yourself as a person, and then rise to your potential, identifying and working at your strengths and weaknesses is necessary.

Using Affirmations to Change Your Thinking

Reprogramming negative thinking can be difficult, but there are ways to help you do so. One of those ways is through using affirmations.

What are affirmations? Webster's Dictionary defines an affirmation as "a statement asserting the existence or the truth of something." In other words, an affirmation is a statement saying "this exists" or "this is true."

Positive affirmations are positive words and thoughts that program your mind, similar to the way a computer is programmed. They help you focus on your goals and your desire. Affirmations create mental pictures in your conscious mind. The mental pictures in your conscious mind then affect the way your subconscious mind works.

It's best and most effective to write affirmations in the present tense. Why, you may ask? Your subconscious mind takes certain things very literally. If you're using an affirmation such as, "I will (lose weight, begin to exercise, etc.)," the subconscious mind may interpret that as, "I'm going to do this someday in the future." The subconscious mind then keeps it as a future goal, not a present goal. In writing and using affirmations, you give your brain a specific direction to move.

Here are a few steps to take when creating affirmations:

- Get alone and find a quiet place where you can think and focus on what you want to achieve.
- Answer the question, "what do you want?" and make the answer as specific as possible. (For example, "I want to lose 20 pounds," rather than, "I want to lose weight.")
- Create a mental picture of the change you want. Visualize a thinner you, or see yourself running a 6K.
- Get a pencil or pen, and write down the goal you are thinking about.

- Write your affirmation underneath the goal. Make it personal
- by starting with words such as "I am. . ."
- If you choose to, include a present tense verb, such as "I show," "I respond," or others.
- You can also add a positive emotion to the affirmation. "I am excited about . . ." for example.
- Finish the affirmation with the results you want. "I am excited about the relaxed person I am becoming."

Repeat the affirmation at least twice a day.

Here are a few examples of positive affirmations:

- I accept myself.
- I believe in myself.
- I am excited about my healthy weight of 165 lbs.
- I have confidence in myself.
- I am a skilled communicator.

How long does it take for affirmations to work? Reprogramming your brain out of negative thinking takes time. And the specific result you are looking for from an affirmation (such as losing weight) also takes time. But your mental reprogramming can begin immediately when you start using affirmations. Your job is to create an environment for them to flourish.

You can choose the way you think. Affirmations are a way to help reprogram your thinking. Try it. You only have your negativity to lose.

Removing Negative Thinking

A person with negative self-esteem generally feels unworthy and unhappy with themselves. Their outlook on life tends to be pessimistic. Negative self-esteem is an uncomfortable feeling to carry around. So, how do you raise your self-esteem? How do you learn to feel happy and pleased with yourself?

First off, what causes self-esteem problems? If you grew up with critical parents, teachers, or other significant adults in your life, that may have an impact on your self-esteem. It's easy to accept what they say at face value.

Some people, for whatever reason, are perfectionists. No matter what they do, it's never good enough. This internal critic can wreak havoc on a person's self-esteem.

Stressful circumstances, such as an ongoing illness or chronic financial problems, with no signs of circumstances getting better, can also contribute to low self-esteem.

Once you've figured out what's causing your low self-esteem, you can start to take steps to raise it.

Here are some ideas:

- Tell your inner critic to shut up. Start thinking about positive parts of yourself ("I have pretty hair, I can play an instrument, I am compassionate towards people.")
- Say goodbye to perfectionism. Recognize that no one can be perfect, and concentrate on "doing well" instead of "doing it perfectly."

- When you make a mistake, think of it as an opportunity rather than a failure. Everyone will make mistakes. Concentrate on what you've learned from the mistake, and give yourself credit for trying.
- Accept what you can't change about yourself. Some parts of yourself (like your height, or past events in your life) can't be changed. Work on seeing the things you can't change from a positive viewpoint.
- Practice taking care of yourself. If a habit is destructive, get rid of it. Seek help if necessary (such as with quitting alcohol or smoking).
- Surround yourself with people who will lift you up, not tear you down. The toxicity of toxic people will spill over onto you if you are not careful. Instead, find people who will support you and build you up.
- Look for ways to help others. Volunteer on a service project, like Habitat for Humanity or other groups that help people. If you're part of a religious organization, offer your time. Groups everywhere look for people willing to help. They will thank you for it, and you will get a feeling of accomplishment.
- If you're dealing with severe anxiety or depression, seek professional help. Having a professional work with you may go a long way towards identifying the roots of your low self-esteem and raising it.

Raising your self-esteem takes work, but it is an effort well worth it.

How to Talk To Yourself for Positive Results

Most of us talk to ourselves all day long, and it's not a sign of being crazy. It's called "self-talk," and it consists of the things we say about ourselves to ourselves.

Unfortunately, a lot of the self-talk that we engage in is negative. What's your reaction if you accidentally burn dinner? Is it, "Oops, there goes dinner for tonight," or, "I burned dinner! I am so stupid!"

Or, let's say you're a college student. You're facing a final exam in a difficult subject. What do you say? "Okay, let me see how much I can study to pass this test," or "I hate this class, I'm no good in it, and I just know I'm going to flunk my final."

In each case, the latter is an example of negative self-talk. Negative self-talk consists of all the negative things you say to yourself. If indulged in for a long period of time, negative self-talk can become toxic. Such self-talk works in the same way as a playground bully, except you are the one that is bullying yourself. A saying goes: "If we talked to our friends the same way we talk to ourselves, we would not have any friends."

So, how do you change negative self-talk? Here are a few steps:

1. Pay attention to what's going on in your head. Write down the things you say to yourself about yourself. This will make you more aware of what you tell yourself. It may be quite a surprise for you to discover how much of your self-talk is negative.
2. Analyze your self-talk. Ask yourself:

- What evidence is there for what I'm telling myself? Is what I'm telling myself true?
- What evidence is there against what I'm telling myself?
- Would I talk to my best friend that way?
- What are some better, more positive ways of viewing the event?

3. Start changing your self-talk. Challenge the way you are talking to yourself. In the examples above, you can say, "Oh, dear, I burned dinner. Next time, I'll set an egg timer, or put an alarm on my watch or phone (or you may come up with another solution) so dinner won't get burned.

Or, with the final exam: "I will study for a certain amount of time. I can ask myself questions about the material. I'll get a study buddy. And even if I do flunk this class, it will not be the end of the world."

Changing your self-talk will take time. Most of us have practiced negative self-talk for years, and becoming aware of our self-talk, analyzing it, and changing it won't happen overnight. But it will happen if you are consistently aware of what you tell yourself, and then analyze and challenge it.

Here's another saying: "Be nice to yourself. It's hard to be happy when someone is mad at you all the time." So, be nice to yourself. Turn the negativity in your head into positive self-talk.

The lives of others: Stop comparing yourself

It is not uncommon to find yourself comparing yourself to others. It is a dangerous thing to do too often. The theory of social comparison has it that we fall into this trap in our efforts to evaluate ourselves. But there is a cost.

Comparison may be a source of motivation and enable growth, but it also can trigger us to fall in a downward spiral to self-doubt.

There are three major reasons why we should fight the urge to compare ourselves to others.

Kill joy

The first is to halt the habit from damaging our own sense of self. Mark Twain was sure that by comparing ourselves we would kill any joy we may have. Research has backed this up finding that it fosters envy, encourages lack of self-confidence, and can lead to depression. It has also been known to compromise our ability to trust our peers.

Of course, looking at how we compare to people who are less fortunate is bound to provide some help to our sense of self, but this has a price too. It may lead to feelings of pleasure in others' misfortunes and so has the capacity to stoke a mean-spirit!

Distorted vision

The second reason we should beware of comparing ourselves with others is because what we see is not always what we get. We could be comparing ourselves with an inaccurate perception.

We all are able to present an edited version of our reality to the outside world. How often do we tell the truth when we are asked how we are doing?

In one recent piece of research published in the Personality and Social Psychology Bulletin, it was confirmed that we are much more likely to demonstrate positive emotion than the negative version. The study also found that we tend to overestimate positive aspects in the lives of others and misread the negative ones.

This means that at one and the same time we are not only comparing ourselves with an unfinished picture of others, but we are twisting the information we receive. We are in danger of feeling insecure because we are comparing how we know we are with how others want to perceive them - not at all like with like.

Don't waste your time

The third reason for fighting against comparing ourselves to others is that it is such a waste of time and effort.

Tearing ourselves apart because we think others look better, have more friends, or are more successful is a motivation killer that makes it harder for us to achieve our goals. By comparing our sense of worth with our perception of others, we condemn ourselves to always be losing.

It is a fact of life that we never reach a point where we are better than everyone else in every way and all the time - so why even consider it? It is much healthier if our focus is on becoming the very best version of ourselves.

Land Of Hope and Glory: How Looking at Things We Have Achieved Boost Self-Esteem

Self-esteem is all about the way we judge ourselves - the way we see ourselves. Some of us believe that the way we look enhances our self-esteem, but the truth is that high self-esteem is a product of our ability to view ourselves as unique and as a result very special the whole time.

A lot of what we think of ourselves is as a result of what happened to us in the past. It therefore follows that a powerful way to underpin our self-belief is to focus on what we have already achieved, what we consider as our past successes. It is our positive narrative.

People like us

A good place to start is to recall that people have found us attractive - girlfriends, boyfriends, wives and husbands. Remember that these people have considered us beautiful and unique and recognised that we have a lot to offer humanity.

Another thing to think about is all the tasks and tests we have passed to get to where we are today. Believe in your mind power and your physical prowess.

It is important to recognize that the way we see ourselves emanates from the power of our thoughts, minds and bodies. It is extremely beneficial if we can use the power of our minds to develop a love for ourselves - in a healthy, not a narcissistic way.

Little things matter

However small they may have seemed at the time, it is a boost to remember those exams we've passed and those races we've won. When we can see ourselves as unique, people around us begin to see us in the same way.

As human beings we are all a mix of positive and negative qualities, but in order to give our self-esteem a lift it is wise to focus on what we have going for us rather than the negative. As often as possible we need to surround ourselves with people who can affirm our successes and not dwell on our failures. By highlighting our positive attributes and surrounding ourselves with positive people, it helps us better accept ourselves and to build our self-esteem.

Look in the mirror

Even when we are alone it is very healthy to compliment ourselves on what we have achieved. It can be as simple as liking the way we have dressed, and how we lost that little bit of weight. Basically every time we do something right for ourselves, it should be recognised and celebrated. If we can learn to do this every day it will become a very positive habit.

A lot of us spend time looking outside ourselves for strength and confidence. But the truth is that these attributes come from within. They are there all the time. We just need to recognise they are there and how they have helped us achieve things in the past. They will do so again in the future.

Don't Beat Yourself Up: Forgive Yourself for Mistakes and Focus on the Positives

Let's face it, to improve the image we have of ourselves it is going to take time, practice and effort. Nothing that is worthwhile is ever going to be easy. Developing good self-esteem is no different. We have to encourage positive and realistic attitudes toward ourselves, the world we inhabit and our worth within it. The root of self-esteem is self-respect.

If we can concentrate in the first place on changing the way we think about ourselves, before we try to change the circumstances we find ourselves in, we can construct our self-esteem. Our goal is to grant ourselves a more positive concept of ourselves, while accepting ourselves honestly and taking down any internal barriers that can stop us from doing our best.

Positive Thinking

There are a variety of methods we can use to convert self-criticism into something more positive, but to focus on them all simultaneously is likely to be overwhelming. Our aim should be to focus on a few at one time and to remind ourselves of these regularly.

As we apply the strategies we choose, we need to strive to be more comfortable with our new ways of thinking.

Life strategies

Avoid exaggeration and head negative thoughts off at the pass: We could start by correcting our internal voice so we stop it exaggerating, especially the negatives – checking ourselves when we tell ourselves we always make the same mistake or that we'll never get a particular promotion.

Tick the boxes and accentuate the positive: It is always good to identify our assets and strengths. We might not have to come up top but we did improve our performance. We may not enjoy giving presentations but we can pat ourselves on the back for trying.

Accept the flaws and imperfections of being human: Every one of us has flaws. They are what make us different. We are allowed to make mistakes – forgive ourselves when they happen. There is a power within this forgiveness that will boost our self-esteem.

Do NOT beat yourself up, give yourself a break: We are who we are and we should celebrate this. Punishing ourselves when we fail is a recipe for keeping ourselves low. Recognize any errors, accept them and move on.

Take Responsibility

Encourage ourselves, don't criticize: Constructive criticism and compliments are more positive approaches than being critical.

Don't play the blame game and don't feel responsible all the time: We are not to blame whenever something goes wrong so, although apologizing and accepting responsibility can be positive, we need to learn to accept, learn and move on. We are not, however, responsible for other people's feelings.

Take responsibility for your own feelings: We can't make other people happy, and we really should not expect others to make us feel good about ourselves. Similarly we should not blame others if we feel guilty or bad about ourselves. Although people may affect our emotions, they don't dictate them.

By using just some of these strategies regularly, we can improve our self-esteem. Focusing on the positives will increase our confidence and ability to make external changes and improve our lives.

Hold Yourself to Account: Set Yourself Some SMART Goals

With new days coming up, we're in a great position to improve our self-esteem – when we make and stick to our achievable resolutions.

Our level of self-esteem reflects the relationship we have with ourselves. The more this is based on respect, trust, affection and interest, the better our self-esteem is bound to be. This doesn't give us permission to look elsewhere when we mess up. It means respectfully and constructively holding ourselves to account.

A good way to do this is to set goals. Our self-esteem is improved when we set a goal and then follow through to make it happen.

We can steal from the world of marketing when setting our goals and make them SMART. This means they need to be Specific, Measurable, and Achievable; as well as Realistic and Timely.

Let us imagine that we don't always do what we say we are going to do. Something seems to always get in the way when we are setting out to pursue our dreams. It is hardly surprising that after a few years of this, we start to feel like maybe we should just give up.

Take that book we all know we have inside us? How many times have we told ourselves that we will start work on it? Goal number 1: get that book written using a S.M.A.R.T. goal!

We could start with our New Year's resolution, but don't make it too vague - "I'm going to write more this year." To be more specific, we could try resorting to write a book. But to ensure the goal is measurable, let us add that we are going to FINISH the book. This would enable us to measure progress and stay on track towards the goal. If it is possible to finish the book then the goal is achievable.

It is important that we make sure our goals are things that can be done without driving ourselves mad because they are unachievable, but we mustn't assume that because something is hard that it can't be achieved.

The question that now needs to be asked about our New Year's resolution is, is our goal realistic? Are we going to be able to find an hour per day to write?

Finally, is our resolution timely? To achieve this goal, what deadline are we going to set? It is important to choose a deadline that is motivating and reasonable. But if it is too soon, it will probably be unrealistic. If it is too far away in the future, it will be difficult to stay motivated.

So instead of a vague "I want to write more" resolution we could settle on the SMART decision of resolving "to finish the book on or before December 31st of this year by writing for 4 hours every Sunday night." Now we have a resolution that is specific, measurable, achievable, realistic and timely. And more importantly, we've made a promise to ourselves to get it done. It is the keeping of this resolution that will enhance our self-esteem.

Beware of Overstretching Yourself: Set Expectations That Are Realistic

When we keep our expectations realistic, it's easy to experience success and feel valuable. But if expectations are set too high or rigid, we can often feel disappointment when they are not achieved. As these disappointments mount, they eat away at our self-esteem.

To ensure our expectations are realistic, start by checking them to determine whether our goals are within reason. Having unrealistic expectations can lead us down the garden path, leaving us demoralized, deflated and even despairing.

Human Nature

It is human nature to want to feel good. We can view ourselves in a positive way; even when it's not realistic.

Types of unrealistic expectations that commonly set people up for failure when they try to change have been identified in recent research studies.

People have been found to reject modest and achievable goals because they believe they are more capable of achieving bigger goals than they really are. In one study of obese women it was found that on average, patients wanted a 32% reduction in weight, when the recommended loss was 5-10%. Even though these women achieved an average weight loss of 35lbs– more impressive than that produced by most weight loss treatments – they were invariably disappointed.

Check Optimism

Many of us are often over-optimistic in the speed of change we expect. Overweight people often begin dieting with high hopes, but after a few weeks we feel defeated by slow progress. This happens with those of us who struggle with other addictions like alcohol abuse and smoking.

It is also common for us to overestimate how much we can improve our lives by making a particular change. The dieters among us, for example, imagine that weight loss will improve lives in many different areas. We expect to be happier, find the romantic partner of our dreams, gain the respect we want, and perhaps even receive a job promotion. These are often overinflated expectations.

What is more beneficial for us to recognize is that it's the pleasure we get from exploring the path to our goals that improves our self-esteem rather than reaching for the goal itself.

A Better Chance

We give ourselves a better chance of boosting our self-esteem when we take caution and spot the ways we may deceive ourselves.

We need to encourage ourselves to move forward, while believing in ourselves and our various plans for change. This can be benefited by reaffirmation of our perseverance and motivation to achieve and maintain our goals, and reminding ourselves of all the problems we are able to leave behind and recognizing the benefits we can enjoy.

The favor we need to grant ourselves is to be realistic in the scope of our expectations. This will help us to be patient during any times when progress is slow; and it will give us the power to put nose to the grindstone if and when we ever suffer a setback.

With realistic and positive perceptions, we can become the people we want to be.

Setting Limits as a Key to Developing Self-Esteem: Agree to What You are Able to Do

Knowing the characteristics of self-esteem and what low self-esteem looks like in the world, it is time to consider how best to accelerate the development of your own self-esteem. One of the best ways to do it is to set reasonable limits for what you can and cannot do. This may seem counterintuitive – wouldn't it lower self-esteem to admit there are things you aren't able to get done? In fact, developing self-esteem means knowing oneself, and setting good personal goals is part of the process.

Have you ever spent much time around someone who has trouble setting limits? Joe might promise his boss that he'll have that report ready by next Monday, while at the same time he promises his wife that he'll take their son to a birthday party on Saturday afternoon and help one friend to move his stuff into his new apartment on Saturday morning. Then on Sunday afternoon he promises another friend that he'll come over and watch the big game with him. All of this could work out if Joe were a really quick worker and could whip the report out in a couple of hours on

Saturday morning. But he takes longer than that to produce quality work.

Joe can't set limits for himself. He doesn't know how, as the saying goes, to say no. Therefore, by the end of the weekend someone is going to lose out. Perhaps his wife and his son, you say? Maybe the friend he'd planned to watch the big game with? In truth, the person who loses in this situation is Joe. When he doesn't get everything done that he has to, or skimps on what he'd promised so that he can get it all in, Joe loses. He probably doesn't lose his job, or his wife, or his friend, at least immediately. What Joe loses is the self-esteem from building satisfaction in doing what he had promised to do. When Joe's usual pattern of behavior doesn't allow him to feel that glow of accomplishment very often, then his self-esteem has nowhere to go but down.

How many Joes do you know? Take a lesson from them, and don't be like Joe. Check those impulses that are found in trying to please everyone. Take a realistic look at what you can do; what you're good at, what you enjoy, and what you have time to accomplish. If you develop a habit of setting some reasonable limits for yourself, it will become easier and easier to do. And if you set goals that you're able to accomplish without running yourself into the ground, you'll enjoy a boost to your daily energy level and to your self-esteem.

Making Commitments and Following Through: Raise Your Self-Esteem with Habits of Excellence

So you've made a decision not to be like Joe. You're working on setting some good limits for yourself on the number and scope of things you agree to do. Now that you're looking at that limited pool of things that are essential or important to you, stop thinking about limits. It's time to think about commitment, and to make it all encompassing.

Commitment is the gauge by which you can measure how well you've done in setting appropriate limits. If you have a reasonable number of things on your plate but you still can't muster a significant level of commitment to them, you may need to revise your limits to include things that are more important to you. If you get up in the morning and have to drag yourself into the shower to start your day, take another look. The kind of commitment you want is the kind that makes you glad that you got up, and feel that the day has good adventures in it.

This is so important because once you have made a commitment to something; you will reap the most benefit from following through. Not only will your task be completed in a way that helps you and others, but you will feel so good about your accomplishments. This is the kind of behavior that will build your self-esteem. Making a habit of such behavior will do you even more good, as you'll find that you get into practice for various kinds of work and for the habits of mind that make following through on your commitments a breeze.

Having decided not to be like Joe, you will benefit richly from a further decision to follow through on your commitments. Self-esteem, you'll recall, grows best when it is grounded in internal motivation and personal responsibility. So when you agree to write a report over the weekend, make sure you plan enough time to make it happen, and then do the job well. You'll be pleased by the recognition you get from others as well as the internal satisfaction you'll feel.

This will continue to motivate you as you move into your next assignment. Soon, you'll realize that you are in a pattern of excellence and that you're having a good time. Your confidence is high, you are basking in the sunlight of positive exposure and recognition, and you have the feeling that you can tackle anything that comes your way. Whether self-esteem is a measure of how accepted you feel in a group or whether you're using it to manage your deep-down fear of death, your habit of following through on your commitments will make you feel better about yourself and increase your self-esteem.

Know Where to Direct Your Focus: Raising Self-Esteem with an Emphasis on the Positive

Much of what lays the foundation for healthy self-esteem involves your skill in such areas as interpersonal relationships and self-perception. Not everyone has equal natural gifts in these areas, and not everyone has the gifts to be a professional athlete or famous author. However, you can increase your self-esteem by developing star power in just one area. If you can become a star in recognizing and playing into your strengths and in keeping your focus on your skills and your accomplishments, then your self-esteem will naturally grow in response.

In so much of modern life, the focus seems to be on weaknesses – identifying them and working to improve these weak areas. We make these sorts of judgments about others, and our performance evaluations tend to take this focus. Is it any wonder, then, that we tend to focus on our own weaknesses? Unfortunately, this is often counterproductive.

Trying to improve in our weak areas can lead to personal growth, but can also trap us in a cycle of negative thinking. The fact is that, no matter how we try; we are unlikely ever going to be as accomplished in areas that don't play to our natural strengths. So if you'd like to be more effective in all aspects of life, and raise your self-esteem in consequence, then concentrate primarily on areas of strength in which you already have a number of skills. Add to your skill base in those areas, increase your competence, and focus on your accomplishments.

When you are at work, take care if you make a to-do list. At the very least, make sure to include on your list any preliminary work that you've already done. This is important because you need some things you can cross off. You will find it very helpful to consider tasks left to do in the context of what you have already accomplished. It's almost inevitable to feel trapped in a long list if you don't keep your focus on what you've achieved. In the same way, sitting around thinking about how you've failed will lead, almost certainly, to more failure.

Your self-talk can have a major impact on the results you can achieve, and certainly on your level of self-esteem. Try to avoid statements that begin with, "I should" or "I must." Though it seems a minor point, your reactions vary based on how you frame a statement for yourself. Here's one way your thoughts might run while engaged in a tedious task: "I should get back to work. I know I'll never finish if I keep getting distracted." Here's another way that will strengthen your self-esteem rather than weakening it: "I would be better able finish this task quickly if I handled it the way I did last week. I polished it off in three hours when I remembered to set a timer for my three-minute breaks. I'll try that again!"

Here's to Me! Self-Esteem Gets a Boost from Regular Self-Recognition and Reward

It's always nice when someone pays you a compliment, and even nicer when someone recognizes the accomplishments you've made through your hard work. Whether it's a quick "I love your new haircut" in the passageway or a bonus check because of sustained effort on recent projects, compliments and rewards make us feel good about ourselves – and they usually motivate us to pursue even greater success. Of course, we can't count on receiving bonuses often, or even daily compliments from others. There are some days when each of us merits more praise than on other days, and sometimes it will come from external sources. But instead of dwelling on a lack of external praise on those other days, cultivate a habit of complimenting and rewarding yourself regularly.

There are people who always frown at themselves in the mirror, either literally or figuratively. There's always something to dislike: "My hair looks horrible today," or "I just can't figure out how to work with this new boss." Instead, find something nice to say to yourself: "I'll be glad when it's time for my hair appointment next week, but in the meantime, I look smashing in this suit!" or "My persistence is going to win the day – I'm learning more and more about my new boss, and soon I'll know how to work with her better." Find the best in yourself. This needn't lead to self-delusion; you can keep a good dose of realism and still put the emphasis on the positive. After all, success breeds success. Pointing out to yourself what you've done well will help you do better still.

Give yourself meaningful rewards on a regular basis, too. Obviously you'll want to scale these appropriately – it wouldn't do much good to give yourself a vacation cruise every time you finish a task at work, and it wouldn't do much for your self-esteem either. As with the child who gets a gold medal or a trophy just for showing up, rewards lose their worth when they become too automatic; they run the risk of promoting an overinflated sense of self-worth when they're out of sync with the level of achievement.

But give yourself a verbal pat on the back when you've contributed something of value to a meeting. Celebrate your successful presentation by taking a friend out to dinner or buy yourself that new novel you've been wanting for a while. Recognizing and rewarding your own achievements will remind you of your own self-worth, and it will give you confidence in your interactions with others and raise your self-esteem as a consequence.

And remember, all of these methods of supporting the growth in your own self-esteem will help you support others as well. Just as self-perception leads us to deeper insights about others, learning for yourself in how to manage the journey from setting personal goals to accomplishments and rewards can lead you to help others do the same and promote their self-esteem in turn.

Maximize Your Self-Esteem by Focusing on Self Discipline

The entire journey to higher self-esteem is not all sweetness and light, and compliments and rewards. In your essential focus on the positive, don't forget to give yourself some accomplishments to focus on by building and exercising your own self-discipline. This is the dose of realism behind your regular doses of compliments and rewards. Success, as we have said, breeds success and your initial achievement of success will require self-discipline.

Even when you have set limits that allow you to commit to the activities that are most important to you, from time to time you will be faced with tasks that don't thrill you. Maybe you have found a job you really care about. Your colleagues are wonderful, the organization's mission is one you believe in deeply and personally, and you even find yourself comfortable in office quarters that some would call Spartan and out of date. There's one major drawback – the 7:30 A.M. start time is driving you crazy. It's nice to get off at 4:15 P.M. and beat the rush hour traffic on the bus ride home, but you live some distance from work and have to get on the morning bus at 6:30 A.M. to be on time to work.

Rather than bailing out on a job that's otherwise perfect for you, it may be time for self-examination and the exercise of some self-discipline. Why does the early start give you so much trouble? Are you in the habit of staying up too late, whether you're reading, out with friends, or even trying to get ahead on your work? A bit of self-examination will reveal what the problem is and, typically, some possible solutions.

There is an equal danger for those who have not developed self-discipline. It may not be that one aspect of an important job gives you particular trouble, but rather that one or two aspects of it interest you far more than the rest, and to the point of distraction. An architect who loves site visits and envisions new structures, but balks at the details of creating blueprints, will not achieve great success without a number of junior partners – and to get those, they need to pay their dues by tending to the details until their visions gain them a stellar reputation.

Here's where the self-discipline comes in – if you want to be happy in your job and accumulate the sort of success that increases your self-esteem, then you're just going to have to change your habits. Perhaps the architect needs to set aside three hours of each work day to do her non-preferred tasks. Perhaps, with your early start, you accept invitations only for weekend nights; perhaps you set an alarm to remind you to go to bed just as you set one to wake up. However it works for you, if you can develop self-discipline and a good set of habits, you'll set yourself up for success in all avenues of life and for the strengthening of your self-esteem.

Reducing Your Stress Level Removes Obstacles to Increasing Your Self-esteem

Stress – we are all subject to it, and everyone experiences stress sometimes. Our response to stress can vary, but it seems that stress stands in our way more often than not. Physiologically, our body responds to stress as a perceived danger, and ramps up production of hormones that put us on alert for a fight or flight response. This is a very useful response to acute stress, whether it was one of our ancestors facing a prowling lion, or one of us suddenly realizing that an automobile accident might be imminent.

However, many people experience chronic lower levels of stress – not imminent danger, but just difficult circumstances that seem to require attention. Once it is activated, we have a difficult time turning off our body's response to stress. While the body is on alert, the mind is liable to overreact to situations, such as traffic jams or upcoming deadlines, and produce the full range of physiological reactions to stress – overkill for the situation, and counterproductive as we try to move forward.

Stress, and chronic stress in particular, has negative consequences for our health. It raises blood pressure, makes us more likely to gain weight, and raises our risk of such conditions like heart attack and stroke. Ongoing stress has probably been associated with nearly every health condition there is. And, it is worthwhile to remember that mental health is part of our overall health as well. A mind that is constantly overreacting to and attempting to deal with stress cannot be at its most healthy, and indeed chronic stress has been linked to numerous mental health conditions as well.

But what does stress have to do with self-esteem? The two have a reciprocal relationship. First, stress affects self-esteem. The typical human responses to stress tend to lower self-esteem – you don't take care of your body because of your stress, so you don't feel like you look or feel as good, so your self-esteem suffers. Or you are paying so much attention to the external stressful factors in your life that you don't take time for the internal focus you need to support your self-esteem. In addition, you are so preoccupied by the stress that you don't maintain your friendships as you mean to, and your self-esteem is thrown off by the changing social situation.

Secondly, self-esteem affects stress. People with higher self-esteem possess more coping skills for dealing with stress. They react better in stressful situations because they have confidence in their ability to handle whatever comes their way. This reciprocal relationship between stress and self-esteem can result in an unfortunate cycle – higher self-esteem would help you reduce your stress, but your stress is lowering your self-esteem. How to break the cycle? Many introspective techniques that can help stop our bodies' stress responses can also be helpful in raising self-esteem. It may be only a matter of finding the will to try one or more of them out.

Use Mindfulness Meditation as a Tool to Reduce Stress and Raise Self-Esteem

If you are wondering how to break the stress/self-esteem cycle and tame your body's responses to stressful events, you should explore the practice of mindfulness meditation. Adapted from several Buddhist principles and practices, it can be a tool that can take you from simple physical relaxation all the way to adaptation of your emotional responses to certain events; what you are able to do with it will depend on your facility with the practice.

In this practice, it is your goal to be mindful of various aspects of yourself – your breathing, the parts of your body, later the sensations of your body, your mental state, and potentially even your emotions – without becoming involved in or distracted by them. It is a practice that teaches you to be mindful and aware without judging, which makes it an excellent tool for the release of stress and the natural increase of self-esteem.

Do not expect too much at the beginning of your practice; make your goal simply to remove yourself from the myriad of thoughts that typically race through your brain and instead focus on your breathing – concentrate on the rise and fall of your abdomen, and the sound your breathing makes. Even success with this small goal may take several sessions; you will find it best to begin with sessions of only a few minutes in length and increase the time as you gain experience. But even if you can't go more than a few minutes being mindful only of your breathing, you will probably end the session with at least a temporary feeling of bodily relaxation and a mind that stops racing with stressful thoughts for a little while.

As you grow in your practice, your mindfulness can extend beyond your breathing. As you become aware of all the parts of your body in turn, it is likely that your posture will improve and you will become aware of all the tension that you store in your muscles. Your mindful meditation will make it possible for you to achieve a physical relaxation and balance that will feed into your mental state. You will begin to let go of your chronic stress, and this will feed your positive sense of self-worth, while allowing your self-esteem to rise.

An expert practitioner of mindful meditation will turn that mindfulness to such difficult areas as mental state and emotions. These are not easy to address because the practitioner cannot be caught up in reliving a story or experience. They also cannot feel the echo of those emotions and have the meditation to achieve its ends. One must notice or become aware of everything without becoming involved. It's a challenge, but the potential reward is great. With practice, a mindful person can predict his or her emotional responses and, for instance, deliberately insert a touch of joy whenever irritation threatens in afternoon traffic. Such self-awareness and self-control, when matched by reduced stress and a positive sense of one's self, will certainly have high self-esteem as its natural outgrowth.

The Big Picture

In the end, whether you're meditating or focusing on your skills and accomplishments, you're not trying to raise your self-esteem for its own sake. It's not as if there is some prize or award for the highest self-esteem in the tri-county area. Rather, high self-esteem is the natural outgrowth of your greater understanding of yourself, your strengths, your desires, and your place in the world.

If you have honestly considered how the components of self-esteem play out in your life, you have made progress toward your goals. If you have examined yourself for signs of lowered self-esteem, considered what the sources of those might be in your life, and done what you can to alter those, you have made much more progress. And if you intentionally add practices to your life that can help promote higher self-esteem, then, well, you should feel good about feeling good about yourself!

LIFE SKILLS

Are You Smiling Yet?

Smile! Has anyone ever caught your face in an awful frown, and said, "Smile?" It may have been the last thing you wanted to do in that moment, but there is a very good reason the social phenomenon of encouraging others to smile is so ingrained in many cultures around the world. Countless studies have shown the benefits of a smile both for the person who is smiling and those who have the pleasant opportunity to encounter their beautiful smile. These benefits are directly linked to our focus: Self Esteem

Smiles have been shown to improve your outlook on life. That little act of broadening your cheeks, curling your lips, squinting your eyes, and maybe even showing your teeth actually affects how you see the world and how you feel about others and yourself. And the bigger your smile, the greater the effect it has on yourself and everyone around you. A major component of self-esteem is how we relate to the world around us, so when we improve our outlook then we are improving our self-esteem.

Smiles also affect the way others see us. People enjoy being around people who genuinely smile a lot. You will be considered more trustworthy, friendly, fun and, yes, attractive. People will be drawn to you if you smile. Are you afraid that your smile looks disingenuous or fake? Don't be. The more you do it; the more natural and beautiful it will become. The smile muscles are like any muscles. They need a good workout to stay sharp. Smile as much as you can in front of the mirror, while watching a movie, sending a text, when you are out with friends and you will be surprised how the smile itself will become more and more appealing to others. When we see others enjoying our company, we feel better about ourselves and we will want to smile even more. And that is a very good thing because now we move on to reason number three.

Smiles cause our body to release the natural feel good chemicals called endorphins. This is solid science and probably one of the reasons humans have developed, over thousands of years, such a love for the smile. Endorphins make us want to smile more because they make us happier and we feel better. Endorphins naturally reduce stress levels, which is something everyone wants. When we are less stressed we can focus and feel more self-assured, further improving our self-esteem.

Finally, smile because smiles are contagious. Let's go back to the introduction when someone said, "Smile!" Without fail, the word is accompanied by a friendly smile upon the face of the well-wisher, and when you see that smile it is nearly impossible not to smile back at this friend, colleague or complete stranger. That is because smiles are contagious. When you smile, others will want to smile with you. You will be helping others receive all of the benefits that we have discussed and more. And by helping others and making the world a happier place, you have just done even more toward improving or maintaining self-esteem.

Stop and Smell the Roses

It is not just the advice of a charismatic gnome you may remember who was pushing his travel site a few years back---and on seemingly every program. This is a philosophy that effects how we see the world around us, ourselves and others.

Life can very easily become one more hurdle to jump after another, one more stumbling block to get past, and one more task to accomplish. Part of our self-esteem is our outlook, so it is important that we stop to take a deep breath and look at the world around us and realize how special little things can be while balancing our daily life.

Find those special things in your life that make you happy, accomplished or sentimental. For most of us it is probably not roses, although they are nice to receive every once in a while. But to improve and maintain self-esteem it is important that our lives do not revolve around rare special occasions. Instead we need to find those special things everyday that make life meaningful and fulfilling to us so our life can feel special and complete.

Find things that make you instantly smile when you see, hear, feel, smell or think of them. Once you find one per day, you will certainly find yourself encountering others. As I am sure you realized; I had left 'taste' out of the list of sensations. While I know that chocolate can very easily make our day special, I encourage you to think beyond the obvious things, like food, towards the more abstract, beautiful and serene.

These special things will be unique to you, but here are a few that you might consider, from the very basic to the more complex. One day it could be a phone call from a friend and the next clean, fresh sheets that you just pulled out of the dryer. It could be a sunset or the sound of birds nesting outside your window. Perhaps it is an act of kindness done to you or by you. It could be spending some quality time with your beloved pet, child or significant other or winding down with an intriguing novel. Perhaps it is writing a love poem or finishing another chapter of your three part novel. It could be jogging or managing to walk one without stopping for the first time in a very long time. How about sipping a warm cup of tea which, if unsweetened, I do not think we would put in the food category, because if you drink hot tea then you know it can be a meditative experience that is just so good for the soul. And lest we forget, be sure to find special things about yourself. Maybe your hair just fell into place this morning or your skin looks radiant or your teeth look extra white. Maybe you lost a little weight or love yourself just the way you are.

I cannot list them all because you must find something new each day. To truly live a life of healthy self-esteem, you must make it your mission to find these things to reflect on, to smile about and for which to be grateful.

What Goes Around

Yes, what goes around truly does come around. Some might call it karma; others might chalk it up to chance. But just as when we help and share with others, we find they do the same in kind. Even a thing such as freely giving appreciation can and will come back to us tenfold. When you make others feel appreciated, they will appreciate you more.

Have you ever experienced feelings of under-appreciation, being overworked or exhaustion? There may be a very good reason for this, and it may just be your own doing, but thankfully, there is a very easy remedy to it. It's not about blame; it's about identifying challenges, facing them head on and finding the solutions.

When we are appreciative of others, they will be more appreciative of us. Self-esteem is closely linked to appreciation. Appreciation, to some extent, represents to us the value that we provide to others through our friendship, our charity, our work, our kindness and every other facet of our being. As we help others feel appreciation for these things and others, we in turn will not just feel more appreciated, but be more appreciated. So, find new ways to be appreciative of the little things that others do to enrich your life and the world around them.

We can very easily find ourselves trapped in our own little world. Appreciation, truly, is thinking of the world beyond what we think and do, and seeing others for the beauty and value they give to our lives. When someone does something special for us, it is very easy to be appreciative, but truly being appreciative of others goes far beyond being thankful for those above and beyond acts of kindness and realizing that there is truly very much we can appreciate in a person.

For example, let us use someone that most of us may never see, but always see the results of his or her actions. This person would be your neighborhood mailman or woman. Does the mailman deliver your mail on time? Does he make sure your mail is securely in the box or tray and not spilling out onto the ground? Do you tend to find your mail dry even on a rainy day? Do your packages appear to have been handled with care? Does she always greet you with a smile? If you find these things to be true, then you have found appreciation for him or her. Now, you might be saying it is her job to do these things and do them right. But the fact is that it's everyone's job to treat his or her fellow man with respect and to do the job he or she is tasked with to the best of his or her ability. And everyone wants to be appreciated. You are no exception. A postal worker is no exception.

Now, think of all of the people you do see every day. The people that you do have an opportunity to appreciate. With everyone you meet, find something in that person to appreciate and you will quickly feel the appreciation returned to you.

Have a Little Fun

Work. Work. Worth. At least I did not say it three times, because we do plenty of it and there is always more to do. Hopefully, you do not find the third word a synonym of the first two. If we are relying solely on our mastery of job, task or skill to maintain our self-esteem and feelings of worth, sooner or later we are going to find our self-esteem on a sandy foundation indeed.

So find things that you love to do for pleasure and fun and do them as much as you can. The benefits of this are boundless. When we are doing what we love then we will see benefits to our mood, our outlook and our health. If some of these actives include a social element, we are also increasing our interactions with others, which have its own benefits. All of these components drive self-esteem.

First, let's talk about mood. The mood, while it seems very psychological, it is largely, but not by any means solely, dictated by a physical function in our body. That function is the release of the chemicals; endorphin and serotonin. Both are released at different stages of activity and both contribute to mood. Endorphins are known by many people as happy or feel good chemicals. When they are released by our body through activities we enjoy, we feel a since of happiness, self-satisfaction and belonging; which we have already learned are major components of self-esteem. Serotonin helps us stay balanced and cool through life's ups and downs and improves our sleeping patterns. When life throws us a curve ball, we can respond better and faster and feel more confidently because these chemicals are in balance. When we are performing activities that release these chemicals, we are affecting our body and minds' abilities to interact with the world in a positive and constructive way.

So, how can doing things that you love to do affect our outlook on life? Think for the moment on the woman-- I am certain you know her -- who can only think of work and nothing more. Does this individual feel fulfilled? It is true that many people claim to love their jobs and many do, but for the most part, if one's life is consumed by work and she is never taking time to play, she is only living half of a life. Her outlook is that life is work and getting work done. She is not experiencing the richness of a full life of balance that drives our self-esteem. She is not seeing how fulfilling play can be and how rewarding it is. She is likely only thinking of the next task that needs to be completed and, in that, she ties up all of her self-worth into one component of life.

When we feel better, health-wise, it will help us regulate our self-esteem. Play activities may have benefits such as strengthening the heart and lungs, toning muscles, reducing stress and lowering blood pressure. Or activities may keep you mentally fit by stimulating and expanding the mind. Either way you are feeling better and looking better and maintaining healthy self-esteem.

Develop a Passion

Passion, amusement, diversion, distraction, and hobby. Whatever we call it, spending time with those things that deserve these descriptions is good for the soul. It does not matter what interests us, but it's essential that something does! We need to be interested in things we can read about, study, research, and engage in. All this effort to pursue something outside of our daily grind simply helps us maintain a sense of "self" that is above and beyond. It saves us a lot of hurt and disillusionment as life goes on.

Hobbies help build our self-esteem because learning new things and mastering tasks will build up our belief in ourselves. Hobbies and passions give us stuff that we feel good about. These outside pursuits also help by connecting us to other people. Most interests are shared and provide ways to connect and meet with people. Shared experience is like a problem shared. It diminishes the pain and enriches our progress. There is plenty of research that shows how important feeling connected and supported is when it comes to self-esteem.

Hobbies make us more interesting people. Current affairs, ornithology, baking, philosophy – whatever gets us excited enough to take time to indulge ourselves in an interest or passion makes us more interesting and that in itself makes us feel good. Having a hobby that we are passionate about relieves stress because it takes our mind off problems we may be facing and gives us extra purpose and keeps our minds sharp. Investing in ourselves is indirectly investing in others around us. Doing things that are focused on ourselves can provide a refreshed perspective that is much needed to re-invigorate our relationships with others, and this is good for our self-esteem and wellbeing.

A hobby supports our concept of ourselves. We all have times where we become confused and aimless and it is then that we rely on an independent self-concept remaining intact to help ease the panic that may accompany this feeling of being lost in life's wilderness.

If we need to recapture this self-concept there's a myriad of ways of doing it: Reading; Horse riding; Exercising; Birding; Walking; Learning to recognize trees and wild flowers; Cooking; Knitting; and Interior design. The list is literally endless. We need to build our self-esteem. Pick up a hobby and develop it.

A hobby, any hobby, gives us something that we can focus on and develop ourselves. It is common for low self-esteem to be triggered by an unhappiness that we are not in control of, which leads to feelings of powerlessness and failure. But a hobby gives us something we can control and improve. Hobbies help make us more rounded by having an additional skill.

By picking up a hobby we can make ourselves feel more like wholesome individuals while simultaneously discovering a place where we can go to concentrate our energy and develop ways of improving and enhancing the way we feel about ourselves.

Reward Your Achievements

When we are looking to develop our self-esteem, honoring our achievements matters. It is not their size that is important. The fundamental thing is that they are acknowledged at all. It is a good way of celebrating that we are growing and making the best of our lives. We should ask ourselves each day: was it a good day? Did we complete a challenging project? Did we learn something new? Did we complete a small step towards achieving a bigger goal?

Did we make and take the time to recognize our achievement? Or did we just move on to the next task without another thought? Celebrating even our smallest successes helps keep us energized and motivated.

Long Term Benefits of Marking Our Achievements

Acknowledging our achievements increases the positive emotions like happiness, self-respect, and confidence. It's good in terms of personal growth, but there is a growing body of research which associates regular cultivation of positive emotions with psychological resilience, well-being, and longer lives.

With achievements coming in all sizes and shapes, some are more meaningful than others. It's a good idea to find ways to create memories around our most important successes. This means that in future when we hit moments of self-doubt or find ourselves facing a tough hurdle we can look back on an almost tangible reinforcement of what we are capable of and how far we've already come.

Among the many ways we can record our achievements are keeping a list as an ongoing record. It not only lets us chart our journeys but helps plan the future. Other ideas include creating a journal of achievement in which we write down each success and give ourselves gold stars; buying a special item of jewelry so that each time it is worn it will remind us of our success; start a collection, which could be anything thimbles, stamps, dolls, spoons, action figures, sports memorabilia etc., and buying something for the collection to celebrate each success.

It is important, rather than mulling over what we haven't achieved, to make it a habit to open our eyes to the value of all that we have accomplished and then reward ourselves with some kind words or some pampering. In the long run, it's definitely not the size of each celebration that counts. What is important is the acknowledgement of our growth and recognition of how we are creating the best life possible for ourselves.

When we feel more like we matter, and that we genuinely recognize our contributions, and that we are vital to achieving our goals, we feel more complete. Recognition is priceless. It is much more than money. It increases our confidence, which enhances performance and so generates greater success. So whatever our achievements each day, they need to be rewarded with some type of recognition. When we do we build a stronger person and a better world.

Take Responsibility

Let's face it. It's often difficult to accept responsibility for our actions. We all like others to have a high opinion of us, but this tendency can wrap us in what is known as "denial." Denial creates false perceptions of self and reflects an inability to accept the truth about ourselves.

This makes accepting mistakes possibly painful. As a result, it's often our first reaction to point the finger elsewhere. This inability to accept responsibility is a direct result of insecurity. But by accepting responsibility and embracing it, we are not admitting to being weak and powerless. We are not risking losing the respect of others. In fact, by taking responsibility we earn respect.

Nobody can be perfect all of the time. Everyone makes mistakes. By accepting responsibility, we accept the blame for our actions and also embrace the responsibility for improving our lives. Responsibility is a measure of our self-worth, our level of security, and a very real sign of courage and strength. This ability to be responsible is empowering.

The Consequences for Ducking Responsibility

Failure to accept responsibility for our actions triggers a series of events that are not beneficial for our achieving goals. Failure to accept responsibility sends to our subconscious negative connotations that can seriously sabotage our progress.

One negative consequence is an over-inflated sense of self that gets in the way of getting along with others. This can also lead us to having unrealistic expectations of those around us, which can lead to us becoming more intolerant of other people's inability to live up to our expectations. This is repellent to our peers! As a result, our relationships suffer and few people want to be around us.

Inability to accept responsibility can lead to feelings of insecurity, which can cause doubt about our abilities, and further undermine our self-confidence. It is a spiral of decline and we can get a reputation of being irresponsible, reliant on others, a quitter, disturbed, hopeless, unhappy, irrational, angry, and defiant or depressed.

Why Is Taking Responsibility Difficult

The causes of an inability to accept responsibility are many and varied but they need to be confronted to be overcome. If it is from feeling insecure then we need to identify the cause of this and recognize that the root is someone else, not ourselves. Was it perhaps because we were raised in a chaotic environment and constantly put down, yelled at, or otherwise emotionally abused?

Is our failure due to arrogance, which may be inherited? Again we need to find a way of putting this behind us. Do we suffer prejudices due to intolerance, racial discrimination, or narrow-mindedness?

If any of this sounds familiar then it doesn't make us bad people. But we need to congratulate ourselves for recognizing these characteristics if they apply.

How to Take Responsibility

By accepting that we have a problem in this area we are taking a big step in the right direction. Now we can do a number of things, like realizing we can't place the blame on others for the choices we make. Now we can accept that it's ok to make mistakes. This will improve our self-esteem.

HEALTHY LIFESTYLE

Introduction to the Secret of Self-Esteem

The processes through which self-esteem is produced are chains of feedback that go both ways, and this is why the physical aspect of self-esteem is so important. There is a Buddhist saying that claims that your thoughts change you, that your mind is "everything" in which you depend, and therefore it stands to reason that you are responsible for your thoughts. Modern science, in the form of epigenetic, has certainly found this ancient creed to be true – for it has been discovered that the power of our thoughts, together with our internal states, has the ability to fundamentally transform our DNA, (which is made up of the building blocks of all life on earth). However, it is no less true that our bodies change our minds. Mind and body are part of one seamless whole, and messages are constantly travelling from the mental to the physical and from the physical to the mental. Having understood this looking after ourselves, and promoting our own well-being and peace, becomes a matter of primary importance.

With a proper understanding and valuation of this deep connection, we begin to see how necessary it is to reach the mind, which is the seat of happiness, by the part of the feedback chain which is most readily available to us embodied mortals – the body. Tapping into the connection between the body and mind we are able to achieve new growth in order to become majestically beautiful as the full grown oak in its prime.

The living of a good life has, since ancient times, been the subject of much philosophical discussion. Since the time of Aristotle our ideas on "eudaimonia," or human flourishing, have come a long way. We now know that health and happiness are holistic and that they spring from a natural source, and that the attainment of inner peace and wellbeing does not depend on us being as cerebral as the old philosophers thought. The Yogis and the mystics had a more appropriate understanding of it as the combined effort of mind and body – an effort towards wellness and integration. If even a dog with three legs can be contented, and even blissful, in its life then surely we too, no matter what difficulties we face, can achieve this state that we so often find elusive.

The Ancients, with their connection to the life giving powers of the earth and her natural rhythms, knew that just as the physical world throbbed with the life of the inner spiritual-world just so did our bodies hum and sing to the tune of the gods. All that was required was the ability to play the body like we would play an instrument, and all this would come flowing out and we would find ourselves energized – energized in much the same way that each morning our bodies are energized by the morning sun. And hence came all the dance, beat and rhythm of human culture.

Of course, it is not necessary to be religious. Atheists and theists are equally able to hone their bodies and tap into the inner life giving spring. We all possess it, for life is not given where life is not.

Exercise and Endorphins: The Tantric Rush of Self-Esteem

Researcher Miriam C. Diamond found in her experiments with rats that the brains of rats differed greatly depending on the quality of their existence. For instance, she found that rats that lived in environments with a lot of opportunity to run around and play had significantly better brains than rats that lived in drab and dreary conditions and had no room in which to run. It is an established fact in modern science now that the brain is not a machine but a growing and changing living thing. It is plastic. It is neuroplastic, and therefore malleable. This fact bears witness to the connection between the different realms, physical and mental-spiritual. Exercise is the key to tapping into this connection.

It is known that exercise releases endorphins. One can see endorphins as being the happy chemicals of the body. When they rush through you they give you something of a high, leaving you pain free and with a feeling of wellbeing. Sportsmen and women have been known to forget everything, all of the distractions and tediousness that so often deplete all our inner resources and sense of self-esteem, in the thrill of the moment. This is the joy, the real joy of the present, that we can, all of us, have and we can have it for so little. We can even have it for just a minute or two a day to begin with.

There is the chemical rush of exercise, and there is also the other, more societal, side of it – we feel better about ourselves the more fit we are. There is the myth of Narcissus, the beautiful youth who stared into the lake, gazing upon himself, day in and day out. For his vanity, he was turned into a flower; the white narcissus. Esteeming ourselves and loving ourselves does not mean that we are like the vain Narcissus. No, not at all – there is a self-love that is healthy and conducive to living the good life, conducive to a wholesome society. This healthy self-love means working on ourselves and working to be fit, while saying to ourselves, "Yes, I am lovable and this is something I have achieved through my own merits, through continual work and effort, and I have a right to be proud." In this there is no sap or sentimentality – only the knowledge that we have achieved, and then throwing up our arms and breathing two lungs full of the clean, well deserved, air.

The road to this healthy respect for yourself, for your own body, is intimately linked to respecting the life giving powers. The ancient Chinese called this the chi – chi is the force that flows through the universe. To begin, you can do a few slow and gentle movements every day in the morning, while making sure to do nothing that is hurried or too much for you. A few minutes, even a few seconds, and by and by it will come – the chi we strive for. You will connect to the life of the trees, to the life of the animals, and it will be a truly totemic experience that will leave you rejuvenated, ready for the day.

Mirror on the Wall

When you love the person you see in the mirror you are on the path to real self-esteem. Again, it does not mean you have to be like Narcissus or like the wicked witch that is Snow White's stepmother. But the façade that is merely the reflection of yourself can lead to a degree of reality for the self that you yourself were not necessarily aware of. Perception affects you – both other people's perception and your own perception. When you are pleased with yourself it will not matter anymore what anybody else thinks of you, but while one is not yet fully in possession of true self-esteem it is helpful to think about the impressions you make. Just wearing a flowery top instead of the gray t-shirt you generally wear can make a big difference in how you are received, and how you receive yourself. Putting on make-up, brushing and parting your hair, doing your hair – all this can result in an enormous boost in confidence. When you do this you will find that you can begin to receive compliments from friends and family, sometimes even from perfect strangers, and your sense of self will be affirmed instead of denied. Everybody needs this somewhat. We encourage children in this way, and later they have enough sense of self to take risks. By receiving flattering comments, our own sense of self is developed, and eventually we acquire enough courage to go our own way, to forge new paths and to walk the road less travelled by. Eventually, one arrives at that place of peace – where all is contentment – the nirvana in which we discover the strength that comes out of the connection with our true selves, the self in which it is not possible to be unhappy.

By paying attention to how you look you will learn a lot about yourself, and this is crucial if you want to send the right feedback to your inner self. Our inner selves are so often in such turmoil. This turmoil, all the trauma of the self, can be alleviated. It is not always easy but it is possible. By first creating only the outer image and appearance of who we would like to be, we can, eventually, become that image. A mere appearance can be transformed into reality – a reality of worth. Amy Cuddy, in her TED talk about posture, says that the advice she gives is to "fake it till you become it." Dressing well, putting on make-up, all this is a start in that direction. So, fake it till you make it. And remember that eventually we reach a place of peace. Many have done it. It is possible for all.

Postures of the Higher Self

In her TED talk, Amy Cuddy shares her insight into human posture – the meanings of different poses, the types of people who sit or stand in this or that way, and, most importantly, how posture serves as feedback to both ourselves and to our audience. Posture shapes how people esteem us and how we esteem ourselves. It is a strange thing that the postures we take on because of the value we place on ourselves have, in return, a confirmatory effect on that sense of value, whether it is high or low.

By changing your posture for only two minutes a day you can change your life. Think of the tiger – a fierce and powerful creature which we respect because of its ferocity. If it shrank like a kicked puppy we would, no doubt, have a different attitude towards it. In a somewhat similar manner, although for us human beings there is no call for ferocity, the way we carry ourselves – the ways in which we sit or stand – determine how others regard us, and in turn how we regard ourselves. If you stand in what is called the wonder woman posture, hands on your hips and face held high, you will begin to feel better about yourself, more confident and comfortable, and therefore more likely to be true to the true you. By seeing the easy relation you have with yourself, others will be more likely to like you. Plus, if you are looking to get hired the probability will be on your side as well.

It will be of immense benefit to you if every day you adopt some simple power poses. People who are happy with themselves do not shrink; they do not curl up into a ball or hold themselves. What they do is expand, stretch, and take up space. Practice these and other power poses daily and you will soon notice that you yourself are undergoing a transformative experience. Remember that you are fluid, like water, and that that which contains you can change you. The body can be life changing.

Overcoming all the negativity that pollutes our minds – the pollution that changes the healthy relationship we should have with ourselves by interfering and coming in between the self and the correct estimation of the self – takes will and discipline, but understanding the intricate and inseparable interwoven net of mind and body makes our endeavor dramatically easier.

Through the power posed, it becomes a living, tangible possibility to embody power and by embodying it becomes, in essence, powerful – realizing the power inherent in the human core. In this way all those who are weary and downtrodden, or simply just suffering from a lack of self-esteem, can come to terms with themselves. They can realize, and know with every cell, that such feelings of worthlessness is not the way things have to be; they can know that we have the power to change. After all, the brain is plastic and malleable – we are malleable – we can overcome all these errors in the ways in which we regard ourselves. If fake smiling can lead to all the feelings of a real smile, fake posing can lead to all the positive and self-affirmative feelings of power.

You Are What You Eat

Since our bodies are this important then it only stands to reason that what we put into our bodies is as equally important. From food we get nourishment and energy, but eating the wrong foods can lead to ill-health and, even if you do not become sick, eating the wrong things do not lead to the optimum level of wellness that is the right of each and every one of us. Without a feeling of wellness, it is a lot harder to have a correct relationship to ourselves.

At this juncture of human history, bad food habits have become the norm and so eating correctly has become something of great importance. Eating too much fat or starch can clog our arteries. Certainly too much fat, or too much processed food, constricts our arteries leading to the lessening of the blood flow which means less blood to the heart, less blood to the brain. Blood has long been believed to be a power of great proportions. The life-giving, energizing, oxygen is carried in the blood. When the amount of blood arriving to the different organs of the body is decreased then our faculties also decrease. This is why we feel dull sometimes after a large and heavy meal.

Eating whole wheat flour, natural unprocessed food, and a variety of vegetables results in the body working as it should. The human gut is more used to these unrefined foods as it has had hundreds of years to get used to them. Fibrous food, because of the way in which it is digested, makes us full before we have had a chance to have consumed too many calories.

You will feel more alive if you eat well and, therefore, more able. Skills and abilities are part of what makes up the sense we have of ourselves and our own value – it is good to know that I can do this, and that I am useful, and fulfilling a necessary function. Having lived up to all your expectations of yourself, providing that they are reasonable expectations in keeping with the nature of your true self, you will feel more comfortable in your own skin. Eating well will enable you to live up to your own expectations, to exercise properly, and to treat yourself with all the care that you deserve.

HEALTHY RELATIONSHIPS

How to Become Happier by Building Healthy Relationships with Others

Happiness and self-esteem are two related emotions people will always strive for consciously or not. And being a topic everyone can relate to and be interested in at some point, it has become a subject of study for scientists, psychologists, and researchers who want to analyze the mindset and evolution behind one's self-appreciation.

As a positive psychology researcher, Christopher Peterson left some relevant contributions for the field regarding self-esteem in relation to one's own relationships with others. His personal motto was 'other people matter.' And as other people do matter, he demonstrated through his studies how one's levels of happiness and self-esteem increase depending on the quality of that person's relationships with other people. And not only Peterson's studies, but studies led by different specialists on the subject have shown the benefits of good friendships for oneself. However, building and maintaining healthy and strong relationships takes time and effort from both parts, and experts on the matter suggest two fundamental actions during the cultivating process: identifying the peers' strengths and qualities, and being empathetic and understanding.

Identifying Strengths

The first point of action when building a relationship with others, experts say, is identifying their core strengths and giving them opportunities for using them. For instance, when someone's core strengths are kindness and creativity, building a relationship through those strengths will make the bonds more solid. Every single person has four or five core strengths that make them real and human, and knowing those qualities from close relatives and friends will make both parties appreciate each other more and, consequently, become happier with themselves. In a healthy relationship, the strengths of the members are the base and focus for inspiration and for bringing out the best in each other.

Walking in Their Shoes

Are we usually as equally permissive to others as we are to ourselves? Do we accept other people's excuses on day-to-day situations when we make the same excuses and expect others to accept them? Another call of action for stronger, healthier relationships with other people and oneself comes from a sense of empathy and understanding. According to self-compassion researcher, Dr. Kristin Neff, people tend to underestimate the circumstances of others while overestimating their own. In this case, it is important to feel compassionate and considerate towards other people's actions before thinking less of them or judging them by their decisions. Dr. Neff pinpoints the importance of giving other people the opportunity to act on their own and putting oneself in their position to understand their situation. This action will result in either feeling empathetic and understanding with the person or offering advice for a better behavior, both of which will help strengthen the relationship and feel more self-appreciated.

Experts on the matter have shown how these two separate actions can help in building long-lasting relationships with others, and the payoffs for identifying qualities and showing empathy for others leads to stronger self-esteem as well. At the same time, people automatically become less self-critical and more self-compassionate and aware of their own strengths.

How to Become Happier by Helping Someone in Need

In the words of Winston Churchill, "We make a living by what we get, we make a life by what we give." Following this wise message, there's no arguing that people who receive are happy and grateful, but on the other hand, people who give have been scientifically proven to become happier after their good deeds. A renowned bioethicist who founded the Institute for Research on Unlimited Love, Dr. Stephen Post, made a thorough study demonstrating how altruism and compassion can reduce depression, stress, and anxiety, while lifting happiness and self-realization.

After several studies, results showed that people who spent money on others were significantly happier than those who spent money on themselves. And even though a small act of generosity might not change the entire course of the world, it will in fact reap off the benefits for both the recipient and the benefactor – a win-win for both parts. And on many cases, more often than not, recipients will want to pay it forward by doing another act of kindness for someone else; creating a fulfilling cycle of generosity where everyone involved will have higher levels of happiness, especially after lending a helping hand.

Theory of the Helper's High: Giving Vs. Receiving

A research from Emory University in Atlanta, Georgia, scientifically proved that it releases endorphins and hormones related to reward and satisfaction. Compared to a receiver, the giver's measurable levels of happiness are in fact higher. This theory that received its name by the same psychologists who defined it, shows how participating in a selfless act of generosity leads to self-realization and self-satisfaction.

However, and apart from the scientific researches on the matter, it's no wonder how someone who enjoys receiving will equally enjoy giving, keeping the cycle alive. Another 2010 study from Harvard Business School measured the levels of self-esteem from people in more than 100 countries in order to demonstrate that the ones who participated in volunteering and charity works had higher numbers on the scale. This all exemplifies how people subconsciously feel better when helping someone else out, and those who are helped out will likely continue the cycle, eventually feeling better as well.

The bottom line is that, scientifically proven or not, helping others makes people feel good about themselves. The feeling of reducing another person's pain, physical or emotional, lifts the spirit of anyone involved, even one who's witnessing the action rather than taking part in it. That explains why watching a movie or reading news about a man doing a good deed or a woman helping someone in need makes people feel better, even when they're not directly contributing to the action itself. It's part of a human emotion to want to serve and to be served. The positive side – as if there were a negative – is that, whether it's giving or receiving, this circle of kindness and altruism is directly related to a higher self-esteem and happiness, leading to a longer and healthier life span.

How Volunteering Boosts Self-Esteem Levels

It might not be a common thought, but helping others with a selfless and humanitarian attitude actually brings a long list of benefits for one's self-appreciation and happiness. Participating in charity events to help a community, organization, or any cause has been scientifically proven to help boost the self-esteem and self-value levels of the benefactors involved. These are some of the most relevant benefits of volunteering, from improving health to building stronger relationships with others.

Benefits for the Mind

Volunteering is often recommended by therapists and psychologists to help improve mental health. Helping others comes with a feeling of accomplishment and self-realization that boosts self-confidence and makes the volunteering have a more positive sense of identity. Especially for people who are going through a difficult situation, volunteering helps them stay motivated and stimulated, turning their own worries and negative thoughts into a more satisfying and optimistic perspective; besides being a new, different activity to boost creativity and motivation, while being helpful to others.

The theory of the Helper's High states that 80% of the people who volunteer or help someone else in any way, feel considerably better and happier. The Guardian posted an article on how volunteering can affect helpers, one of them Cally Edwards, who is living proof that the Helper's High theory is real. She volunteers as a birth and post-birth supporter for struggling mothers, and according to her, "It's the feeling that you really have helped someone, that makes it so worthwhile."

Benefits for the Body

Depending on the type of volunteering work, most of them involve some kind of physical activity outdoors, which can be beneficial for the health. Besides all the emotional and mental advantages, several studies have shown that volunteer work can also improve the life span: it reduces the chances of heart diseases, lowers blood pressure, improves memory, and reduces any muscular pain, according to experts.

Benefits for Social Skills

Building new, healthy relationships is proven to boost self-confidence and self-esteem, and volunteering is an effective way to do so. When working for a common cause, people relate and create a bond that improves social skills. In addition, volunteers connect in a special way to the community or organization they're dedicating their time to, which can also be a great way to build powerful networking and bring benefits to their personal and professional lives.

Last but not least, developing social skills and creating a community of close people will lower the chances of depression to a great extent. As one of the main symptoms of a low self-esteem, depression can occur when there's no social interaction or contact with others, and by volunteering, the chances of feeling isolated are almost nonexistent. Therefore, participating in charity events and volunteering cuts out any signs of depression, while lifting self-esteem.

Whether it's a healthier body, a peaceful mind, or better social skills and relationships, the truth is that volunteering brings numerous benefits to becoming more self-appreciative and happier. Not only helping the community, the animals, or the environment in need, but helping yourself to live a healthier and better life.

Help! Because No Man Is an Island

One woman said to her friend, as they were standing in the bus, how happy she was when she came home and found that Joe, her husband, had vacuumed the carpet while she was away and taken out the trash. It had been a relief. That is what she said. She ran her hand through a tendril of hair, and curling it about her fingers, she remarked, "It was such a relief." She was a businesswoman running a big company, she had conferences to go to and it was just such a relief to find that she could go home and just relax without having to worry about the chores.

"No man is an island, entire unto himself." Thus spoke John Donne, poet of the sixteenth century, and these words of his are as true now as they were when he first uttered them so long ago, once during a dim and darkened age. Now, centuries later, here we are with all the comforts of progress and the innovations of science. Our lives have become, in many ways, easier and pleasanter than those of our ancestors. But the important things – friends and family, love – are still the truly important things.

And yet, we so often make the error of behaving as though we were indeed islands – each one of us a separate and self-sufficient island – but because the fact is that we are not self-sufficient acting in this way, inevitably leads us crashing into the wall of the real world; the wall of how things actually work.

Our family and our friends are our own circle and they are the people we depend on. And they depend on us too. It is as though there is an energy flow that is shared where we all become stronger and more capable of standing by this sharing of energy. This energy can be disturbed, however, if someone is unkind or uncaring. If, for instance, someone never does the dishes or if a friend is sick and one never bothers to ask how she is then the energy becomes disturbed and all those feeling of peace, of being at home and being ourselves, disappear.

Little things matter. Vacuum sometimes, buy flowers, cook a meal, and take out the trash. When you hear that a friend or a family member has a problem simply say that you are always willing to listen, and tell them you are there if they wish to talk. Remember that none of us are islands. We all need a helping hand sometimes or a shoulder to cry on. Friends and family are affiliation groups from which we receive affirmation for our own sense of self. This goes both ways – they receive affirmation from us also. When we do not show our depth of caring then others may feel that they are unworthy. We have to show them that it is not so. So roll up your sleeves and wash the plates in hot sudsy water. There are so many ways to help – fix your mother's computer if you are a computer geek, cat sit while your friend is away, or drive a carless friend to work.

Don't Put a Sock in It

Were you ever told in school, because you spoke out of turn, to "put a sock in it?" Well, it is time now to take the sock out of it. As long as we say nothing that is impolite, or something that undermines someone else's legitimate differences, it is a good thing to speak up. Speaking up is a trait we should all encourage ourselves to have, whether we are at work or at school. Have you heard the song by Simon and Garfunkel called "The Sound of Silence?" If, by whatever chance, you have not already heard it then have a listen – it is an old classic. "Silence like a cancer grows. Hear my words that I might teach you. Take my arms that I might reach you." These are some of the words of this song.

We all have something to share. We have all had thoughts and experiences that no one else in the universe has had. If these things are never said then no one will ever benefit from the individuality that is you. We are all here trying to be decent, trying to do the right thing, and to leave the world just a little better than we found it but that will never happen if we put a sock in our mouths and stay shut up. We all need to be open. Openness is the virtue of the day. Look at the light and how open it is. We must endeavor to be as open as the light. That is the only way that we will all be enlightened. Think to yourself of all the human effort it took to reach the point we are at now, and none of this would have come to be if everybody had been silent, if nobody had spoken or done anything. We would never have had the indubitable benefit of the automobile or the aero plane. Charles Darwin would never have written his seminal work On the Origin of Species. Albert Einstein's theory of relativity would be unknown to this day, and democracy and freedom of speech, and all the values of the "Universal Declaration of Human Rights," would not have come to pass. The world would be poorer in spirit, its growth stunted and disfigured.

To not speak, to not take advantage of the years and countless years of sheer work and effort that it has taken to reach this stage where we can begin to speak without constantly being censored, would be to disrespect those pioneers who paved the path for us.

And just think of all the wonderful things that can result from one word that someone hears, and one word that someone says. These things can be both life-changing and game-changing. Both at work and at school, or at a university, speech is necessary. At school, participation is part of the grade. Also speaking out, raising your hand, drawing attention to yourself develops your sense of self, and adds to your prowess. No error, no mismanagement, can ever be fixed if no one mentions it. And then there are the brilliant ideas – society is about sharing of ideas, and we respect both ourselves and each other when we open up and are willing to discuss our ideas.

The Unique You

Everybody is different. Your difference is something to be happy about. You are an individual, and there is nobody else who can be what you are. Comparing yourself to that girl in class who everybody thinks is perfect is pointless. She may have been popular but you know you have other qualities – you can take a joke and you know that life is more than just grades. You know that it is a dull Jack who works all day and never plays. Of course, we must not be too hard on that perfect girl who is, after all, also a unique person and has gifts and talents, all sorts of qualities, which you do not possess. But that is the important thing – to remember our differences and celebrate.

Think about your own talents. What are you good at? What do you enjoy? What do you derive the most pleasure from? What are your goals and dreams? People may tell you that you should be this or do this, but there is no need to conform to any of these expectations unless you really wish to, unless their hopes for you match your own hopes for yourself – the authentic and true yourself, not the mask that so many of us put on for others. Only you know what is best. Sometimes, usually because we have not lived truly, not lived in the way that our core selves demand, we do not know what suits us. You will see the university student who goes from course to course, unable to settle down. Such a person is often someone who has suffered a crisis of the self and does not know what his or her passions are.

Passions are important. Your passions will fill you with joy, they will make you want to live, to wake up and greet the day, to seize opportunities. Passion will make you live spontaneously. Passion will make you live in the moment. Whatever your passion is – be it fashion designing, or in being an entrepreneur, or in writing the best, most moving, poetry you can possibly write – it will be something individually tailored to fit your wants and desires. It can take some time to discovery but the discovery is well worth the wait.

When your birthday comes you celebrate the unique and beautiful person that is you. But in between birthday, in all the ordinary days, it often slips our mind – how special we are. But we are all special. You are special, and nobody and nothing can take the shine out of you.

How to Boost Your Self-Esteem with the People around You

We're constantly reminded how happiness and self-appreciation come from within, but there are numerous external factors that have an influence on how we feel about ourselves and how our emotions can change. With all the inevitable difficulties and challenges we face during our living years, it only makes sense that we surround ourselves with people who make us feel good and happy, instead of those who are dragging us down and adding more pain. Every single person in this world will eventually go through a rough time or simply have a bad day, and having people with negative thoughts, constant criticisms or judgmental opinions won't make it better. Psychologists have proven how people around us can have a strong influence on how we feel, and being surrounded by your close ones who support, admire, and love you can only bring a sense of self-confidence and joy.

Measurable Happiness Lies on Social Relationships

According to the British Household Panel Survey, a research study clearly showed that "an increase in the level of social relationships and connections is proportional to an income bonus of $100,000 a year in terms of life satisfaction;" while those same changes in real income don't show such high levels of happiness. So, it's safe to say that it has been scientifically and statistically proven how strong, healthy relationships with your close ones – and not so close – are so much more worth than an unlimited credit balance. On one hand, being surrounded by your close ones enhances creativity, energy, and relaxation; all in one. Doing activities with your friends, talking to coworkers, or eating dinner with your relatives keeps your mind active and increases the chances of recording more positive thoughts than negative ones. In this way, working on your relationships with other people creates a feeling of motivation and enthusiasm, resulting in you feeling better about yourself in the long run.

On the other hand, people who know your qualities and strengths will be more likely to enjoy your time together, help in moment of crisis, and know how to lift you up when the circumstances require so. Your close friends and relatives are the best people to know how to make you feel better and make you smile. Those who lift you up will also need you to lift them up when the moment arrives, so there's a sense of reassurance knowing that having someone's back will eventually result in a more positive life for yourself. The Harvard Medical School professor and psychiatrist, George Vaillant, once stated "the only thing that really matters in life are your relationships to other people."

However, relationships with others don't necessarily mean your best friends and family, but strangers too. Studies have shown how helping others will boost positive feelings. Volunteering, helping a neighbor, or smiling to people on the streets is a great way to lift others while increasing your self-esteem. Either way, being in touch with other individuals, sharing experiences together, and knowing someone has your back has an incredibly heavy influence on how you perceive yourself.

SEEKING
PROFESSIONAL HELP

Low Self-Esteem: When to Seek Professional Help

Self-esteem is crucial to how we see life and how we perceive ourselves, and whenever it's low, we might need to make some changes in order to acquire a healthier and happier take on life. Before seeking professional help, it's key to know whether the patient will benefit from it or become unmotivated. Depending on the age and the patient's desire to get help, there are some things that parents, relatives, and friends can do to help the patient become more self-confident. The Counseling and Mental Health Center recommends some actions that might help overcoming the issue.

- Constant appraising and overcompensating might not be realistic, but pointing out the strengths and positive qualities of the people with self-esteem problems might make them feel better. Especially with children, setting a good and positive example for facing struggles might help.
- People with low self-esteem need to step out of their comfort zone and constant routine to change the negativity in their lives, so encouraging them to try new activities and learn new things is always beneficial.
- Whenever they make a mistake or come up with a pessimist attitude, it's important to let them know it's OK. Instead of letting them get frustrated, try to point out the positive side in every situation.
- When they're kids or teens in school, focus on their successes rather than giving relevance to a subject they're failing or any other struggle they might be facing.

- Interpersonal relationships are proven to benefit self-esteem, so encourage them to make new friends and meet new people by joining clubs, volunteering, or any other activity that involves a positive environment.
- When people are struggling from within, chances are they might need to express some repressed feelings with people they're comfortable with, so it's essential they have someone, whether it's a best friend, coworker, or parent, to whom they can express thoughts and emotions.

These are all things that family and friends can do to help a person with low self-esteem. However, when the person is having hard time adjusting to day-to-day activities, developing new skills and learning, or when there's any sign of self-harm or suicidal attempts, professional help needs to interfere. There are many help centers and therapists that can tackle the problem with more expertise. For under-aged patients, parents will have to make the decision and take them to see a specialist, but in the case of adults the decision to get help has to come on their own, so there's a need for even more support from his/her close ones.

Seeking professional help is always the best way to treat and solve the problem, regardless of the level of gravity. Yet it's not always easy to make the person want to get help, especially when self-esteem is the main issue. So, in order to make the patient feel comfortable, supported, and loved, the strategy will have to be a step-by-step process in which both the people around them and professionals will have an important role.

Emotional and Behavioral Disorders

Once self-esteem issues have been detected, the patient will ideally seek professional help to overcome them, and probably the question they or their parents ask themselves is where to look for an expert take. There are many different options, from life coaching to a personal therapist, or even a more specialized health center. Depending on patients, their ages and their level of gravity, one might be more recommended than the other, since all of them attack specific issues. The right moment to look for this kind of help is when patients experience chronic depression, attention deficit, self-destructive thoughts, and most of all, self-harm and suicidal attempts.

Specialized Centers and Services

The internet offers a wide variety of information about specialized centers for mental health that have confidential support services by telephone or online. If the patient is under the age of 25, a youth counseling service center might be ideal, since they only work with teenagers and develop a series of approaches and techniques appropriate for these ages. The Young Minds Parents Helpline is one good option for parents concerned about their child's emotional health. The helpline offers free support, helpful information and advice regarding emotional and behavioral problems. The most referred health centers for children and teens in the U.S. are the Center for Emotional Health of Greater Philadelphia, the Center for Emotional Health of North Carolina, the American Academy of Child and Adolescent Psychiatry, the National Federation of Families for Children's Mental Health, and the National Association for Children's Behavioral Health.

For adults, there are organizations and associations for people who need a different approach. The National Association for Self-Esteem's main mission is to integrate self-esteem as part of every American individual and to build resilience to help cope with difficulties in a more positive way, and they do so by offering products to help defeat the member's issues such as self-help and self-development books, parenting books, manuals, guides, and useful communication kits. On the other hand, the UT Counseling and Mental Center provides counseling, therapy, and psychiatric services for students and families struggling with these kinds of mental or emotional disorders. The UTCMC has a Crisis Line to address more urgent situations such as suicidal crisis, personal emergencies, etc., to which patients can call any day of the year to receive immediate help from a trained specialist. Other helpful specialized centers include the National Empowerment Center, the Department of Health and Human Services, and the Anxiety and Depression Association of America, all of which offer general assistance to personality, behavior, and overall mental disorders.

Most communities have specialized centers that help people with chronic illnesses, addictions, and emotional and mental disorders, whether they're the patient or patient's families and friends. And regardless the specific aim of the organization or center, they're most likely to help directly or refer to a more suitable help service to work with regularly. Either way, people can always find support and guidance within their own communities.

How to Treat It Professionally

The different treatments for low self-esteem and self-confidence vary depending on many factors such as the patient's age, disposition to be helped, interpersonal relationships, mental conditions, and so on. Knowing what specific help to be sought is crucial for treating the situation the best possible way. So, whether it's cognitive therapy, coaching and counseling, or the attachment approach, the patient has to be prepared and know which technique will help faster and more effectively.

Treatment through Cognitive Behavior Therapy

Probably the most recommended treatment for self-esteem patients, the Cognitive Behavior Therapy, or CBT, is a specialized approach as a form of psychotherapy to help treat a variety of mental and emotional conditions. Its aim is to provide a thorough outline for understanding the causes of the problem. When using CBT, psychologists focus on behavior through thoughts and emotions, offering new communication and interaction skills and analyzing the results of these developed skills on self-perception. One advantage that Cognitive Behavior therapists offer is building new self-confidence and self-esteem based on the patient's strengths and qualities, which make them get in touch with their more positive mindsets and eventually feel better about themselves.

Treatment through Counseling

A counselor can be of great help for knowing the underlying factors and motives. He/she will analyze the patient's behavior to try to understand the main reasons for having self-esteem issues, in order to choose the best strategy to overcome them. Whether it's person-centered, individual counseling or group counseling, the expert can help the patient cope with emotional and mental struggles, look for new alternatives, and feel better after several sessions. Through counseling, the expert provides a safe and comfortable space for the patient to explore negative thoughts and experiences while suggesting actions that result in a more positive thinking.

Treatment through the Attachment Theory

Lastly, there's one approach that has been proven to help patients with self-esteem. This technique aims to describe long-term interpersonal relationships psycho-dynamically. According to the Attachment Theory, an enduring relationship with another human being can help a person with low self-esteem feel more appreciated and cared for. In this way, the approach analyzes the relationships of the patient and establishes a connection of trust between them in order to create a positive bond. This is especially helpful for younger patients who can work their issues through the attachment to their parents.

Overall, these treatment approaches offer patients a solution and escape to their emotional struggles, but the most important thing to take into account for truly effective results is treating the patient with an approach he/she feels comfortable with. Patients with self-esteem problems can be easily frustrated and unmotivated, which makes it more likely for them to not want to get help. However, a patient who feels safe and comfortable around the therapist or counselor will probably overcome the issue faster, so it's essential that the chosen approach not only tackles the problem, but also makes the patient less resilient to get better in time.

Alexandra Strong

Developing Self-Esteem

Made in the USA
Middletown, DE
02 August 2016